INSIGHT POCKET GUIDES

KV-579-215

MILAN

APA PUBLICATIONS

Part of the Langenscheidt Publishing Group

L

MANI

EMPORIO ARMANI

Genève · L. Léman · Lausanne · Schwyz · LIECHTEN-STEIN · Salzburg · WIEN

Annecy · Montreux · Interlaken · SWITZERLAND · Wildspitze · Innsbruck · Großglockner · AUSTRIA

Mt. Blanc ▲4807 m · M. Rosa · Locarno · P. Bernina · 3772 m · Brenner · 3797 m

4634 m · 4049 m · Ortler · SOUTH TYROL · Lienz · Plöckenpass · Graz

Grenoble · Aosta · Lugano · Como · 3899 m · Bozen (Bolzano) · Villach · Klagenfurt

Mt. Pelvoux · L. di Como · Trento · Udine · Loibelpass

4103 m · Novara · Bergamo · L. di Garda · Verona · Pordenone · LJUBLJANA · SLOVENIA · Zagreb

M. Viso · Torino (Turin) · MILANO (Milan) · Mantua · Padua · Venezia (Venice) · Trieste · CROATIA

3841m · PIEMONTE · Alessandria · Parma · Chioggia · Rijeka · Karlovac

Cuneo · Savona · Genova · Piacenza · Modena · Ferrara · Pula · Banja Luka

Grasse · MONACO · EMILIA-ROMAGNA · Bologna · BOSNIA AND HERZEGOVINA

Cannes · Nice · San Remo · La Spezia · Ravenna · Zadar

Mediterranean Sea · Pisa · Bellaria · Rimini · Split

FRANCE · Livorno · Firenze (Florence) · SAN MARINO

TUSCANY · Pescara · Adriatic Sea · Maribor

ELBA · Siena · Arezzo · Perugia · Dubrovnik

Bastia · M. Amiata · ITALY · Terni · Gr. Sasso d'Italia · Ancona

Corte · CORSE (CORSICA) · 1738 m · Grosseto · Viterbo · LATIUM · L'Aquila · ▲2914 m

Ajaccio · Civitavecchia · ROMA (Rome) · ABRUZZO · Vieste

Bonifacio · Latina · S. Severo · Foggia

Porto Torres · Olbia · ISOLE PONZIANE · Napoli (Naples) · Vesuvius · Bari · UGLI

Oristano · SARDEGNA (SARDINIA) · Salerno · CAMPANIA · Potenza · Brindisi

Iglesias · Cagliari · Tyrrhenian Sea · Taranto · Lecce

Mediterranean Sea · CALABRIA · Cosenza

ISOLE EOLIE · Crotone

Bizerte · Trapani · Palermo · Messina · Catanzaro

Marsala · Reggio di Calábria

TUNIS · Caltanissetta · M. Etna · 3340 m

J. Serj · Nabeul · Agrigento · Catania

1357 m · Gela · Siracusa · Ionian Sea

Kairouan · Sousse · SICILIA (SICILY)

TUNISIA · MALTA · Valletta

Sfax

N

Italy

160 km / 100 miles

Welcome!

Milan confounds many people's romantic image of Italy and 'La Dolca Vita'. The country's biggest metropolis, it is *the* centre of commerce and industry (from fashion to automobiles) and the pace here is fast. But that isn't to say it has no appeal for the tourist in search of cultural attractions. Important since Etruscan times, and in the Middle Ages the leading city in the Lombard League, Milan offers many fine buildings, art treasures and museums, plus a superb cuisine.

In this book, Insight Guides' correspondent in Milan, Umberto Troni, brings you the best of Milan in a series of tailor-made itineraries. He begins with three full-day tours combining the essential sights, such as the Duomo, S Maria delle Grazie, containing Da Vinci's *The Last Supper*, and the Castello Sforzesco. These are followed by 10 Pick & Mix itineraries focusing on Milan's less celebrated attractions and then three excursions taking in the abbeys of the Bassa Milanese, Pavia and Bergamo. Complementing the itineraries section of the guide are ideas on shopping, eating out and nightlife, a calendar of special events and a fact-packed practical information section.

Umberto Troni first went to live in Milan to work with the theatre director Giorgio Strehler. A Venetian by birth, he has been an admirer of Milan ever since his first glimpse of the city's huge Stazione Centrale, which, he says, wouldn't be out of place as a backdrop in Verdi's *Aida*. Milan still makes his pulse race, and in this guide he aims to share his enthusiasm with some of the city's many visitors.

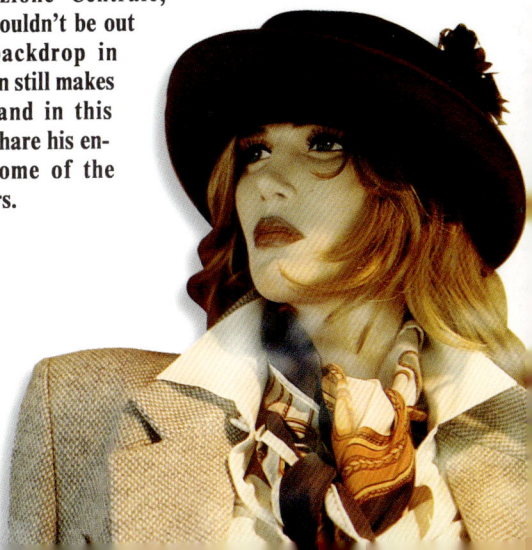

C O N T E N T S

History & Culture

From Milan's early days as an Etruscan settlement through the years of the Lombard League and the Risorgimento and ending with the corruption scandals of the 1990s **10**

Day Itineraries

Pick & Mix

*Pages 2/3:
two gods: fashion
and the Church*

Pages 8/9:
La Scala
Opera House

SENSO UNI

HISTORY

The City in the Middle

Milan, or *Milano*, derives its name from the Celtic 'mid land', and the city's origins stretch back to the 4th century BC when the Celtic tribe of the Insubres conquered northern Italy.

The Romans, who conquered Milan under Consul Marcus Claudius Marcellus in 222BC, named the place 'Mediolanum', because Milan, strategically situated as it is in the Padana Plain, links the Italian peninsula and continental Europe. Milan thus became an important military base on the north-western border of the Roman province of Cisalpine Gaul, which soon embraced the whole of Upper Italy.

Leonardo da Vinci, 'Musico'

The collapse of the Roman Empire into its two halves meant that Milan acquired the status of capital of the Western Roman Empire between AD286 and 402. It was the second largest city in Italy after Rome itself. Moreover, Emperor Constantine's Edict of Milan, issued in 313, made the city the capital of Western Christendom; and after the arrival from Trier of St Ambrose (339–97), bishop of Milan and the city's patron saint, Milan played a decisive political role.

Archaeological finds at S Sepolcro and in the Via Nerino, as well as at

Culture

the Porta Romana and the Porta Ticinese, reveal that the Roman city was originally laid out in a square plan.

After the fall of Rome, in the 6th century, the epoch of the Lombards began; however, their kings chose Pavia as their capital, and Monza as their summer residence. And Milan? Three centuries later, in 1176, it was once again very prominent and in a position to inflict defeat on Emperor Barbarossa. During this period the Basilica of S Ambrogio was rebuilt and served as a model for every other Romanesque structure in Italy – the Basilica of S Eustorgio and the Abbazia di Chiaravalle being just two examples.

Antonio Pollaiolo, 'giovane donna'

At the end of the 13th century, the Visconti family and its heirs became the supreme lords of Milan. The city grew rich and the Gothic architecture of the *Duomo*, the cathedral, became a symbol of Milan's revival. The city's trading connections extended across Europe to London – Lombard Street dates from that time.

In the mid-15th century the Sforza family took over from the Viscontis and began constructing the Castello Sforzesco. Milan reached the high point of its prosperity during this period, and attracted famous artists such as Leonardo da Vinci and Bramante.

At the end of the 15th century Milan fell to the French, and in 1525 to the Spanish-Austrian Habsburg empire of Charles V, whose financier, Tommaso Marino, began the palace in the Piazza della Scala (today it is the seat of the municipal authorities) in 1539.

In 1565 the Milanese archbishop S Carlo Borromeo created the

11

The Piazza della Scala around 1880

very first social institution for the poor of the city, while Federico Borromeo laid the foundations of the famous Pinacoteca Ambrosiana. In 1630 the city suffered an outbreak of the plague.

In 1714, after the Peace of Rastatt, which brought the War of the Spanish Succession to an end, Milan became part of Austria. The Milanese bourgeoisie developed, craft and manufacturing flourished and the city was once again visited by great artists: Tiepolo, for example, who did the frescoes for the Palazzo Clerici. Austrian Empress Maria Theresa promoted the arts and created an efficient administration. The Accademia di Brera, the Orto Botanico and the Osservatorio Astronomico were all established. The Teatro alla Scala was the masterpiece of Neoclassical architect Piermarini; Maggiolini started the Milanese tradition of furniture design, and dell'Appiani created frescoes to adorn the houses of the wealthy.

In 1796 Napoleon occupied Milan and built the Foro Buonaparte and the Arco della Pace. In 1815, after the Congress of Vienna, the Austrians returned and stayed until 1859. During these years the Italian liberation movement known as the *Risorgimento* found its fullest expression in the operas of Giuseppe Verdi, which were a huge success at La Scala.

After the unification of Italy, Milan became the industrial, financial and business capital of Italy. It began to outgrow its 17th-century Spanish walls. The first workers' tenements sprang up to the north, around the factories of Falk, Breda and Pirelli, and work began on such monumental public buildings as the central station and the city cemetery. The old canals, the *navigli*, were filled in, and the first ring-roads were built above them.

After World War I the focus of industrial development shifted away from metalworking and rubber to the automobile industry, Alfa Romeo, Isotta Fraschini, Bianchi, and Magneti Marelli being just some of the notable names. In a climate marked by strikes and lockouts, and by clashes between workers and employers, the Partito Nazionale Fascista, founded by Benito Mussolini in 1919 and financed by industry, gained ground steadily and eventually came to power in 1924. During the Fascist period the city expanded rapidly, and in 1943 it numbered one million inhabitants.

At the end of World War II, Milan very soon reassumed its leading economic role. New housing estates and office blocks – the Stazione Garibaldi is a typical example – were built in the areas of the city that had been destroyed. The Pirelli building, erected in 1955, is the symbol of this rebirth.

In the wake of this economic development, Milan became a popular destination for immigrants from poorer regions, in particular Southern Italy. Luchino Visconti's film *Rocco and his Brothers* (1960) portrays the difficulties encountered by a rural family attempting to adapt to the alien world of the big city. This influx of new social groups contributed greatly to the 'Italian economic miracle' of the 1960s. It was also during these years that the Piccolo Teatro of Giorgio Strehler and Paolo Grassi first began to make a name for itself.

By the end of the 1960s, Milan's destiny was being shaped by political struggles. The so-called 'hot autumn' of the trade unions in 1968 was followed by the *anni di piombo*, or 'leaden years', during which the struggle of the *Brigate Rosse* (Red Brigade) against the 'system' reached its climax with the death of the publisher Feltrinelli. A supporter of the terrorist left, Feltrinelli died while attempting to blow up a high-voltage transmission tower.

After this, municipal policy was determined by various coalitions headed by Bettino Craxi, the kingpin. However, it was in Milan that the 'Tangentopoli' (Bribesville) scandals first erupted in 1992, with a Socialist Party official accused of taking bribes (*tangenti*) for a public works contract. Antonio di Pietro, magistrate and reluctant hero, spearheaded the *Mani Pulite* ('Clean Hands') campaign until his resignation in 1994. But the investigations continue and have exposed corrupt practices ranging from the awarding of Milan's metro contracts to allegations of financial irregularities within the Milan-based media empire of Silvio Berlusconi; even the glamorous image of the Milanese fashion industry (the city has overtaken Rome as Italy's fashion capital) has been tarnished.

Corruption and maladministration have taken their toll on Milan, with the flames fanned by the separatist Northern League. Recently Milan has suffered from economic stagnation and political gridlock. However, Albertini, the new mayor, is a technocrat, committed to running the city

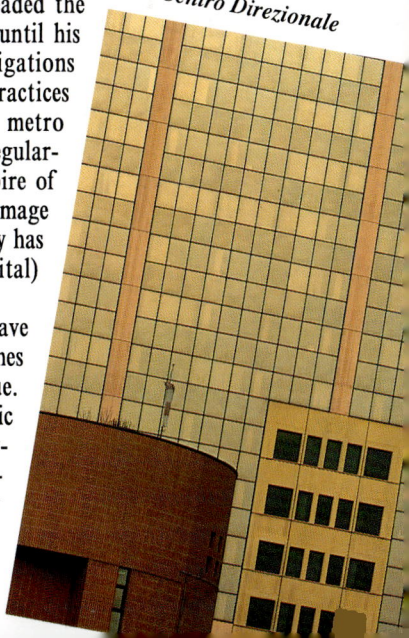

Centro Direzionale

like a commercial enterprise. Milan's mayor has pledged his administration to revitalise the city. Let us hope it is not *lungo come la fabbrica del Duomo* ('as long as the building of the cathedral'), as a popular Milanese saying has it, expressing a world-weary grasp of Italian realities.

The Future of Milan

Although the population of the urban heart of Milan has been decreasing since the mid-1970s, Greater Milan, *la grande Milano*, is clearly becoming more congested. Thirty years ago this conurbation was still a flourishing agricultural area, but today the 200 municipalities that make up the *Provincia di Milan*, and which have since been absorbed by the big city, are suffering from the resulting infrastructure problems. The Milan Metro, with barely 50km (30 miles) of rail, is totally unable to cater for any meaningful portion of the city's 500,000 or so daily commuters. Nor are there enough bus and taxi lanes. The result of all this is that streets are now jammed with private cars, there are queues everywhere, and the people endure stress and smog. Since the 1970s, Milan's city council has repeatedly failed to get its traffic and development plans approved. However, recently strides have been made in the right direction with the creation of pedestrian zones.

The busy Corso Buenos Aires

Meanwhile, the population in the city's historic centre has increasingly had to make way for new offices and apartment blocks. Milan's famous and traditional hotels are being transformed into luxury residences housing the top managers of the city's big firms, who pay astronomical rents to stay there, while their families enjoy fresh air and tranquillity out in their villas on Lake Como – all of them luxury commuters who drive out of the city at weekends, when others are not driving in.

This phenomenon of 'the exodus of the rich' – actually quite a recent development – has meant that Milan has lost considerable taxation revenue, since the Italians are taxed according to where they live. Even major, internationally-known firms such as Pirelli, Alfa Romeo and Magneti Marelli – Milan's pride and joy as well as the city's main sources of revenue – are relocating outside the city, where they can create their own efficient infrastructures: IBM alone has provided 2,200 jobs in Segrate, to the northwest of the city.

Hopefully the practical and constructive minds of the Milanese will retain the upper hand even in this delicate situation, and succeed in preserving the city's humanity.

Historical Highlights

6th century BC Milan founded by the Etruscans.

396 Celtic tribe of the Insubres over-runs early Etruscan settlement.

222 Milan taken by Rome.

AD286–402 Milan becomes capital of the Western Roman Empire.

313 Constantine the Great issues the Edict of Milan, granting tolerance of the Christian faith.

374 St Ambrose (Sant' Ambrogio) elected bishop of Milan.

1097 Birth of the *Comune di Milano*, Free City of Milan, with its own independent charter.

1162 Milan captured by Barbarossa.

1176 The Lombard League, founded in 1167, composed of the cities of Upper Italy and led by Milan, defeats Barbarossa near Legnano.

1277 The Viscontis become the lords of Milan. Their coat-of-arms portrays a serpent with a Saracen in its mouth.

1450 Francesco Sforza, son-in-law of the last of the Viscontis, is made Duke of Milan. The city then flourishes under Ludovico Sforza, 'Il Moro' (1479–99).

1499 Milan occupied by the French under Louis XII.

1525 After the victory of Charles V over the French near Pavia, Milan becomes part of the Habsburg empire.

1556 Partition of the Habsburg empire: the Duchy of Milan now belongs to Philip II of Spain.

1630 Outbreak of the plague in the city, vividly described by 19th-century writer Alessandro Manzoni.

1714 War of the Spanish Succession ends. Milan becomes part of Austria, and flourishes under Empress Maria Theresa.

1796 Milan occupied by Napoleon.

1815 Milan becomes Austrian again after the Congress of Vienna. The *Risorgimento*, and the flowering of Milanese opera and theatre, gather pace.

1859 Milan becomes Italian. The city becomes the nation's industrial and financial capital.

1918 By the end of World War I, the city has 700,000 inhabitants. First labour disputes take place.

1919 In the Piazza San Sepolcro, Mussolini announces the foundation of the Fascist Party. Marinetti's Futurism triumphs in the artistic salons.

1924–40 The city's population rises to one million during Fascism.

1943 Milan suffers serious damage during Allied bombing raids. First *piani regolatori* (development plans) are drawn up for the city.

1946 After the war, Milan once again emerges as the capital of Italian industry.

1955 The Pirelli building, symbol of the city's rapid reconstruction, is erected.

1957 Construction work begins on the Milan Metro. Lack of town planning leads to the destruction of old parts of the city. Dormitory suburbs spring up, unfortunately not connected to the Metro.

1968 Political unrest manifested in student demonstrations and the 'hot autumn' of the trade unions.

1970s Red Brigade terrorism.

1992 'Tangentopoli' – the corruption scandals come to light in Milan.

1992–5 *Mani Pulite* ('Clean Hands') campaign, spearheaded by magistrate Antonio di Pietro, endeavours to eradicate the 'kickback' scandals.

1995 Maurizio Gucci murdered in Milan.

1997 Gianni Versace murdered.

1998–2001 La Scala's historic opera house closed for renovation.

Anyone who understands Milan understands Italy. Far more than Rome, Florence, Venice or Naples, Milan is a true cross-section of all things Italian, with its magnificent historical and cultural heritage, its cultural and human interest, its urbanity and its architecture. Milan may be defined as the business capital of Italy; and it is also the most European of all Italy's cities. A permanent rival to Rome, the political capital, Milan remains the reference point for Italy. While Rome discusses, Milan acts. But Rome does create the economic framework within which Milan has to act, much to the grief of many Milanese managers forced to commute to Rome and haunt its antechambers in order to obtain permits and licences.

View from the Duomo

Milan is the centre of high finance and of economic and industrial power. It is also the headquarters of the country's private television stations, its press and advertising agencies and its fashion designers. On top of that, the city also possesses the best higher education establishments and the best university structures in Italy.

Milan is laid out in the shape of a star around the Duomo, and its industrial and suburban sprawl extends out towards Como, Varese and Monza in the northwest and towards Bergamo in the northeast with the new technopolis of La Bicocca. The city has also spread southwards over the past few years, evidenced by the weird-looking skyscraper estates at Gratosoglio or the small garden cities of Milano Fiori or San Siro.

Even though the construction work in the city is often bad, Milan is now taking a belated interest in renovation, and its historical quarters still retain their character.

The visitor will be amazed by the sheer tempo of everyday business life here, and by the inimitable readiness with which festivals are celebrated. Evenings tend to be spent in the city's 50 cinemas, in its 45 theatres where plays, music and cabaret can be enjoyed, or in its literary cafés, its typical *osterie* (rustic restaurants) and its discothèques. Particularly fruitful sources of the city's rich social life are the Piazza del Duomo, Corso Vittorio Emanuele, Via Torino, the Brera, and the Navigli-Porta Ticinese district.

Immigrants add to the cosmopolitan feel of Milan: Black Africans, North Africans, Filipinos and Chinese work as domestic staff,

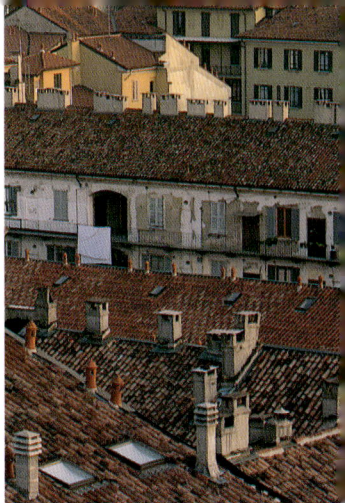

Rooftops in the Navigli area

sell smuggled cigarettes on street-corners and also run small shops selling exotic goods. Out in the suburbs clashes between locals and Albanian immigrants are on the increase. But sooner or later this new workforce will be integrated too; Milan has always understood how to learn from its immigrants, how to live from the ideas and the energy of those eager to work.

Milan never stands still: it keeps on changing and renewing itself, and that applies not only to urban development here but also to the lifestyle of its inhabitants. Look the Milan of today in the face and you'll sense the eagerness with which it faces tomorrow.

Understanding the Milanese

A lot of cities welcome strangers with open arms; more prejudiced ones reject them. Milan rather tends to put its freshly-arrived visitor to the test and, if he passes, accepts him. Should he fail, however, he gets rejected.

The Milanese are open-hearted, cheerful, outspoken and very responsive to strangers. This is why we recommend the visitor to be both open and inquisitive. The search for knowledge is the fount of creativity, and it's almost sacred as far as the Milanese are concerned. Adapt to the Milanese and you are sure to be readily accepted by them.

The Milanese are intuitive and generous. The expression *El milanès el ga el cör in man* (rough translation: 'the Milanese wears his heart on his sleeve') didn't originate by accident. The people are also thoroughly reliable, both at work and in private. A visitor who is open and has nothing to hide will discover an equally open and many-sided Milan. For this reason Milan is the only really cosmopolitan city in Italy – a genuine melting-pot.

The city has changed enormously over the past 30 years. The industrial era is long gone, and with its service-based

A genuine Milanese

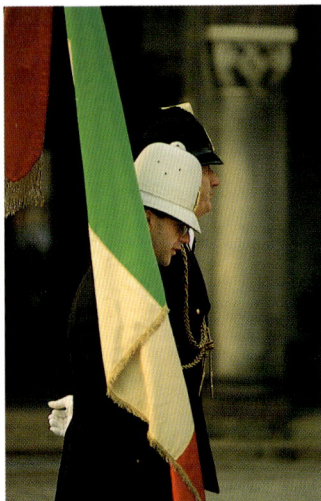

True service

society Milan is now at the cutting edge of European progress.

The average Milanese gets out of bed at 6.30am, drinks an *espresso* (very few Italians have a proper breakfast), and then listens to the news in the bathroom, paying special attention to the Tokyo stock market report (the Milanese adore stocks and shares). Then it's off to work, bumper to bumper, into the smog and stress (every morning 300,000 drive in, 90,000 drive out); the Metro only slightly alleviates the situation, and the buses get stuck in the traffic jams too.

And every morning you will come across the *vigile del traffico, 'Il Ghisa'*, the traffic policeman, with his elegant uniform and elegant gestures, setting things right with shrill blows on his whistle. *Ghisa* is a nickname, so do avoid saying *scusi, signor Ghisa* to him; the correct version is *scusi signor vigile*.

The *Ghisa* is both loved and feared, and this becomes most evident during *Epifania* (Epiphany) when the Milanese, who have received mountains of traffic tickets throughout the year, heap up great piles of *panettoni* (Milanese cake baked with lemon rind and sultanas) at the feet of the aforesaid guardian of the law as he stands at his road junction, to thank him for the difficult and wearing task he is forced to perform. That's typical of the Milanese: they're generous and *simpatico*.

Daily at midday, the hectic rush spreads to the bars: people eat standing up in a *tavola calda*, though not without having had a swift *aperitivo* beforehand. The bars in Milan provide all kinds of different snacks – olives, *crostini al salmone, crostini alle verdure, patatine* – all of which can be accompanied by a Campari, a Zucca, a Martini or a Prosecco. Conversation revolves inescapably around the *Weekend*: the seaside, the mountains, the holiday home, skiing, sailing, Paris, or the latest exhibition in Venice or Florence. The Milanese are always on the move, and eager to see

Time for a Campari

things and experience new sensations – the very act of travelling is relaxation for them!

Then in the evening there's *cena alla casa* (supper at home) or perhaps in a restaurant in the company of friends. Some people visit *La Scala*, the world famous Milan opera. In 1998 *La Scala* embarks on an ambitious restoration programme, leaving its historic home for La Bicocca, an industrial zone. The company is scheduled to return to its home in 2001, when it will stage an operatic celebration of Verdi to mark the centenery of his death.

The social structure of the city is, however, not as homogeneous as it once was. These days Milanese liberals are protesting against the moribund municipal administration which treats immigration with apparent indifference and seems to have no plan for finding jobs and accommodation for the newcomers.

Getting your Bearings

Milan is laid out in the shape of a star, with the Piazza del Duomo at its centre. The old ring of the *navigli* – ancient canals which were once navigable, but are now filled in – surrounded the medieval city.

A second ring, laid out when the walls dating from the Spanish period were torn down, reveals the extent of urban expansion in the 16th century, though it also encompasses the green open spaces of the Parco Sempione and the Giardini Pubblici.

Most of the important things that happen in Milan take place within these two rings. Taking centre stage are the Piazza del Duomo, the Galleria Vittorio Emanuele and the area between Via Dante, Via Manzoni and Corso Vittorio Emanuele. But the extension of the latter, the Corso Venezia, which continues beyond the Porta Venezia to become the amazingly straight Corso Buenos Aires (and later, at the Piazzale Loreto, leads on to the motorways heading north), also plays a leading role in the elegant world of the fashion industry and high finance, the two gods which are the very backbone of Italy's second city.

The northern part of the city is its industrial heart, while the south is predominantly residential, with such satellite towns as Milano Fiori and Milano 3 in Basiglio.

Milan

500 m / 547 yards

Corso

Piazzale Damiano Chiesa

S.Idefonso

Via Gattamelata

Via Giovanni da Procida

Ospedale d. Bambini V. Buzzi

CIMITERO MONUMENTALE

Via Procaccini

Piazzale Cimitero Monumentale

Via Carlo Farini

Stazione Porta Garibaldi

Viale Lu

Via Francesco Albani

Viale Eginardo

Velodromo Vigorelli

Industria

Via G. Mussi

Via Paolo Sarpi

Via Luigi

Viale Montello

Viale Crispi

Porta Gariba

Garibaldi

Via

Sempione

Via Melzi d'Eril

Canonica

Corso

Moscova

Via Stauto

FIERA & CAMPIONARIA

Piazza Italia

Via

Via Monte Bianco

Via Monte

Via Cassiodoro

Canova

Via Masseno

Piazza Sempione

Corpus Domini

Porta Sempione

Via Legnano

Arena

Acquario

S. Mar

Via Correggio

Via Rosa

Piazzale Giulio Cesare

Via Vincenzo Monti

PARCO SEMPIONE

Viale Gadio

Foro

Via Legnano

Via Piazza Castello

Palazzo di Bre

Palazzo Cusani

Via C.

Piazza M.Buonarroti

Via Tiziano

Buonarroti

Via L. Mascheroni

Palazzo dell' Arte

Viale Gadio

Bonaparte

S. Maria del Car

Via Correggio

Ravizza

Via Michel

Via

Mario

Via XX Settembre

Via Vincenzo Monti

Stazione Nord

Castello Sforzesco

Largo Via Cusani Cairoli

Teat alla Sca

Piazza Piemonte

Corso

Vercelli

Via Cimarosa

Piazzale Baracca

Cenacolo Vinciano

Foro Buonaparte

Carducci

Palazzo Litta

Corso Magenta

Palazzo Clerici

Piazza Sicilia

Via Elba

Via Paolo Giovio

Corso

Magenta

Via Meravigli

Posta

Via Sardegna

Washington

Viale di Porta Vercellina

Palazzo delle Stelline

Via San

Vittore

S. Ambrogio

Palazzo della Borsa

Ambrosiana

Viale Ergisto Bezzi

Piazza Vesuvio

Via Cappucio

Via Torino

Museo Naz. della Scienza e. della Tecnica

Università Cattolica

Piazzale Tripoli

Via Giorgio

Via Boni

Piazzale de Agostini

Foppa

PARCO SOLARI

Viale

Coni

Zugna

Papiniano

Via Edmondo

Via Ausonio

Palazzo Trivulzio

S. Lorenzo

Via Misurata

Via Vincenzo

Via

Via Andrea Solari

Porta Ticinese

Corso Porta Genova

Porta Genova

Via Molino delle Armi

Via Leone

S. Maria del Rosário

Via Savona

Anfiteatro Romano

PARCO DELLE BASILICHE

Piazza Napoli

Via Andrea Solari

Bergognone

Stazione di Porta Genova

S. Eustorgio

S. Maria d. Miracoli

Via Tolstoi

Via Savona

Via Tortona

Darsena

Viale Gorizia

Piazzale XXIV Maggio

Viale Gian Galeazzo

Corso Italia

Univer Co Boc

Via Tortona

Naviglio Grande

Porta

Ticinese

Corso S. Gottardo

Via

Via Savona

Naviglio Grande

Ripa

di

Segantini

Via E. Tabacchi

S. CRISTOFORO

Viale

S. Cipriano

Viale

Cassala

Viale

Liguria

Via G.

Viale

Centrale d'Latte

Tiba

SOLA

Via Galvani

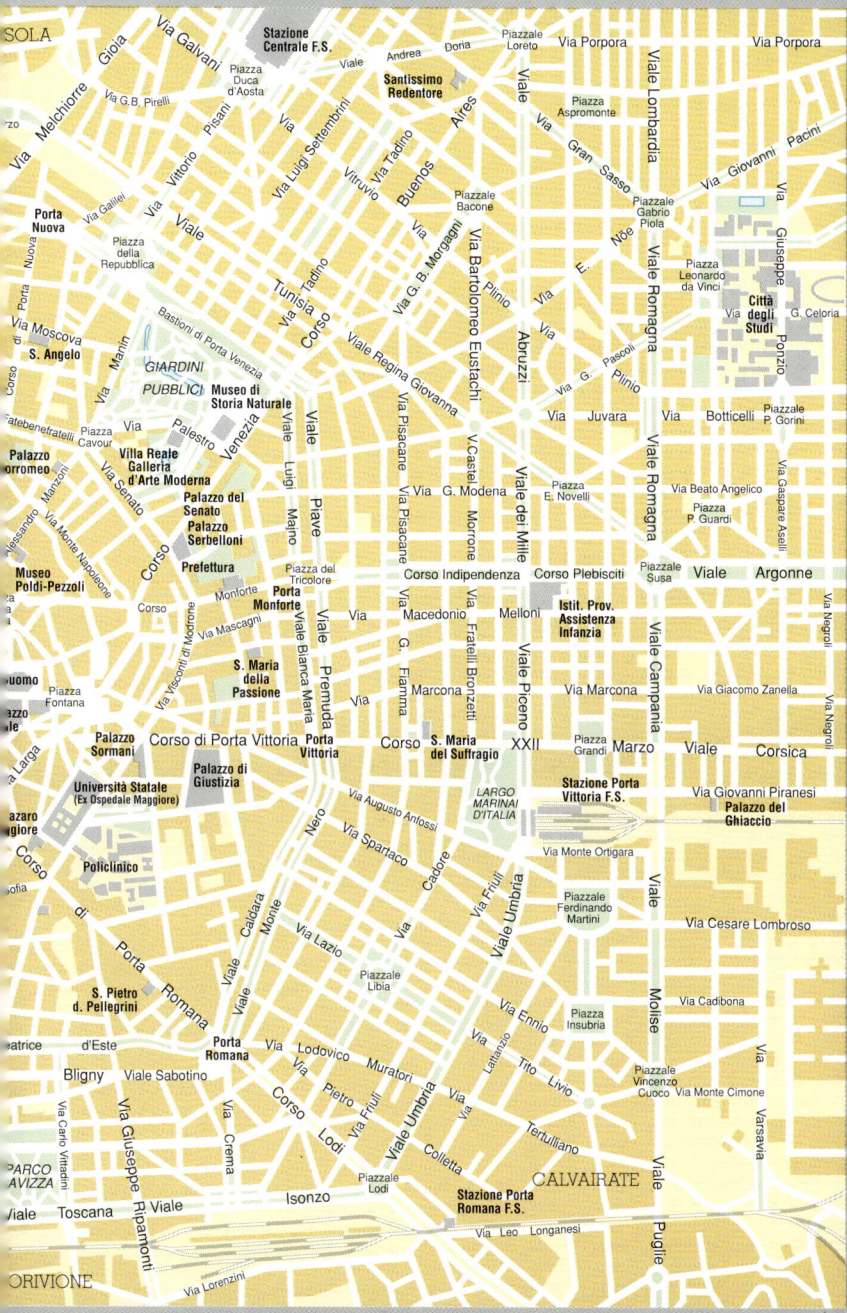

Stazione
Centrale F.S.

Piazzale
Loreto

Via Porpora   Via Porpora

Gioia

Via G.B. Pirelli

Andrea   Doria

Piazza
Duca
d'Aosta

Santissimo
Redentore

Viale

Via

Pisani

Via Luigi Settembrini

Vittorio

Vitruvio

Via Tadino

Buenos

Aires

Piazza
Aspromonte

Via

Gran Sasso

Viale Lombardia

Via Giovanni

Pacini

Via

Porta
Nuova

Via Galilei

Viale

Via

Piazza
della
Repubblica

Tunisia

Corso

Via Tadino

Via G. B. Morgagni

Via Bartolomeo Eustachi

Viale Regina Giovanna

Piazzale
Bacone

Plinio

Piazzale
Gabrio
Piola

E.

Nöe

Via Romagna

Piazza
Leonardo
da Vinci

Città
degli
Studi

Giuseppe

G. Celoria

Ponzio

Via Galilei

Via Moscova

S. Angelo

Martini

Via

Bastioni di Porta Venezia

GIARDINI
PUBBLICI

Museo di
Storia Naturale

Venezia

Viale

Abruzzi

Via

Via G. Pascoli

Plinio

Via Juvara

Via

Botticelli

Piazzale
P. Gorini

Corso

Fatebenefratelli

Piazza
Cavour

Via

Palestro

Luigi

Piave

Via G. Modena

V. Castel

Morrone

Piazza
E. Novelli

Via Beato Angelico

Piazza
P. Guardi

Via Gaspare Aselli

Palazzo
orromeo

Manzoni

Via Senato

Villa Reale
Galleria
d'Arte Moderna

Palazzo del
Senato
Palazzo
Serbelloni

Majno

Via Pisacane

Viale dei Mille

Piazza
E. Novelli

Museo
Poldi-Pezzoli

Alessandro

Via Monte Napoleone

Prefettura

Piazza del
Tricolore

Corso Indipendenza

Corso Plebisciti

Piazzale
Susa

Viale   Argonne

uomo

Corso

Monforte

Via Mascagni

Porta
Monforte

Via

Macedonio

Melloni

Istit. Prov.
Assistenza
Infanzia

Viale Campania

Via Negroli

Piazza
Fontana

Via Visconti di Modrone

Viale

Fratelli Bronzetti

G.

Flamma

Via

Via Marcona

Via Giacomo Zanella

azzo
e

S. Maria
della
Passione

Premuda

Viale Bianca Maria

Marcona

Viale Piceno

Via Negroli

Palazzo
Sormani

Corso di Porta Vittoria

Porta
Vittoria

Via

Corso

S. Maria
del Suffragio

XXII

Piazza
Grandi

Marzo

Viale   Corsica

Larga

Università Statale
(Ex Ospedale Maggiore)

Palazzo di
Giustizia

Via Augusto Anfossi

LARGO
MARINAI
D'ITALIA

Stazione Porta
Vittoria F.S.

Via Giovanni Piranesi

Palazzo del
Ghiaccio

azaro
ggiore

Policlinico

di

Nero

Via Spartaco

Cadore

Via Monte Ortigara

Viale

ofia

Porta

Romana

Caldara

Monte

Via Lazio

Via Friuli

Viale Umbria

Piazzale
Ferdinando
Martini

Via Cesare Lombroso

Molise

Via Cadibona

S. Pietro
d. Pellegrini

Viale

Piazzale
Libia

Via Ennio

Piazza
Insubria

atrice

d'Este

Porta
Romana

Via

Lodovico

Muratori

Via

Lattanzio

Tito

Livio

Piazzale
Vincenzo
Cuoco

Via Monte Cimone

Bligny

Viale Sabotino

Crema

Corso

Via

Pietro

Via Friuli

Viale Umbria

Via

Tertulliano

Varsavia

PARCO
AVIZZA

Via Carlo Vittadini

Via Giuseppe Ripamonti

Viale

Lodi

Colletta

Viale

Puglie

Viale

Toscana

Isonzo

Piazzale
Lodi

Stazione Porta
Romana F.S.

CALVAIRATE

ORIVIONE

Via Lorenzini

Via Leo   Longanesi

Day itineraries

DAY 1

The Old City

From the Gothic pinnacles of Milan's Duomo to the music of Verdi in La Scala. This is a full-day's tour on foot, beginning at the Piazza del Duomo, and continuing via the Palazzo Reale, the Museo del Duomo, the Galleria Vittorio Emanuele II, the Teatro alla Scala and the Museo Poldi-Pezzoli, to the Palazzo Clerici.

– Tram 1, 4, 8, 15; Metro M2/3 to 'Duomo' –

For all of us here in Milan the **Duomo** is far more than just a church: it is a symbol of the city, and the *Madonnina* on top of its highest pinnacle, shining golden against the sky, accompanies ev-

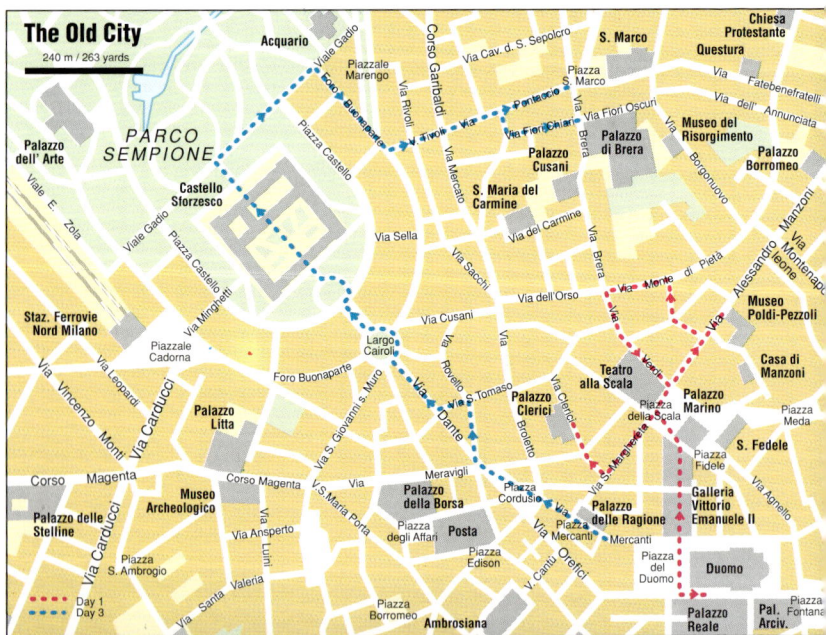

The Old City

240 m / 263 yards

Day 1
Day 3

ery Milanese on his travels – *O mia bella Madunina*. The massive cathedral nevertheless conveys a strong sense of lightness, especially because of those pinnacles decorating its facade. Work on the Duomo began in 1386 and has never really stopped since: the Milanese refer to their cathedral very aptly as the 'factory', because the last of its five gigantic bronze doors, the work of sculptor Minguzzi, was only finally completed in 1965.

If you include the highest pinnacle it is 109m (350ft) high, 157m (500ft) long and 92m (300ft) wide. Built of pink-tinged Italian marble (which has only recently been liberated from its grey coating of exhaust fumes), the Duomo is the third largest church in Christendom after St Peter's in Rome and Seville cathedral. It can house more than 25,000 people. There are over 3,000 statues clustered together on the facade and on the roof, and you need to go up 500 steps in order to reach the terrace – don't worry though: lifts are also available (look for the sign saying *ascensori* at the left-hand entrance).

Structural alterations, above all during the 15th century at the hands of S Carlo Borromeo, have not detracted from the sheer splendour of its Gothic architecture. You will be overawed by the majesty interior of

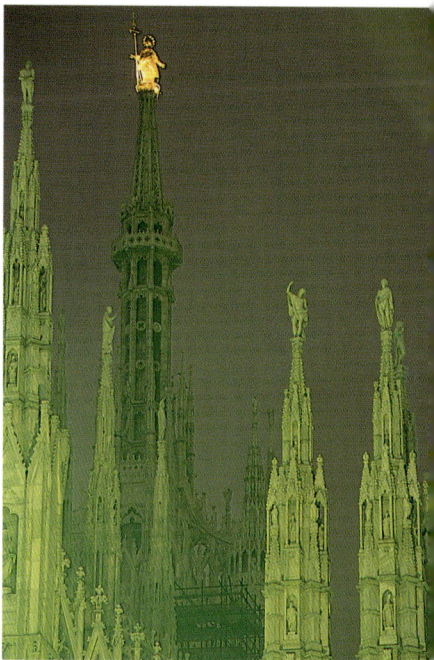

Milan's Duomo and the Madonnina

the Duomo, and if you sit alone in the half-darkness of one of the five naves and let your gaze wander across the milky light penetrating the magnificent windows, and along the mighty columns all the way up to the ceiling – if possible during a celebration of early morning mass – you will understand something of the overpowering mystery of the place.

The **Tesoro del Duomo** (Treasury, open 9am–noon and 2.30–6pm) is situated on the right-hand side of the rear choir. Archbishop Ariberto's Evangeliary can be admired here. The chapel of S Carlo Borromeo is also worth a visit – the gold mask on the sarcophagus is particularly impressive.

Keep an eye out for an astronomical curiosity: from the left nave, where a sundial with a Capricorn symbol can be seen, a narrow brass strip runs across the floor, crossing the entire cathedral and ending on the right side. Light falls directly on this strip through a hole in the roof twice annually, on 21 June and 21 December, and the system was once used to keep time.

To reach the roof, first take the lift and then continue upwards on foot until you finally reach the feet of the *Madonnina*. Here it's easy to get lost among the 700-year-old pinnacles, and there's a fantastic view of the city and the nearby Alps to be had – only on certain days, however, when the wind is in the right direction, otherwise the Milanese panorama tends, unfortunately, to be cloaked in a comparatively thick layer of smog.

Back down at the bottom, you can begin your walk through central Milan. To be perfectly honest, the **Piazza del Duomo** really is rather ugly despite the great fountains: the 1943 bombardment destroyed nearly all of the old buildings around the cathedral square – these are currently being renovated. Today's building facades are, moreover, 'adorned' by even more unpleasant-looking neon signs. And Mussolini's ugly Palazzo dell'Arengario, situated right next to the majestic Duomo, clashes dreadfully with it. However, the Palazzo dell'Arengario does contain the *Azienda Promozione Turismo* (*APT*) (**Tourist Information Office,** open 8am–7pm, tel: 725241), where you can find out the current situation regarding the *La Scala* opera house.

Behind the Arengario is the **Palazzo Reale**, built by Piermarini, the architect of La Scala. This building, commissioned in 1770 by the Austrian empress Maria Theresa, today houses magnificent exhibitions, and also contains the **Museo Civico d'Arte Contemporanea**

Galleria Vittorio Emanuele II

(open daily except Monday, 9.30am–5.20pm). Having taken a look at the extensive collection of contemporary Italian art and sculpture here it's worth going back to the cathedral once more to visit the **Museo del Duomo** (daily 9.30am–12.30pm and 3–6pm). Here, an informative collection, covering 20 exhibition rooms, documents the history of the building.

Afterwards you must bid farewell to the pigeons and the Japanese tourists, as well as to Vittorio Emanuele II on his horse in the middle of the square, and plunge into the world of the **Galleria Vittorio Emanuele II**, the finest and most exclusive shopping arcade in all of Italy. The southernmost of the Galleria's four 'arms' connects the Duomo with La Scala. Here you'll find numerous super-chic shops (especially bookshops) and fashionable restaurants along a distance of 200m/yds. And it's in the Galleria that you can have your first *aperitivo* of the day – an Italian ritual, performed once before lunch and once before going home in the evening. On the corner, on the left of the entrance to the Duomo, is the famous **Camparino**; it is named after the Campari family, inventors of the aperitif. So, how would you like your Campari: straight *(liscio)*, or with soda *(al Selz)*? No question about it: Campari definitely needs to be drunk with soda, but first the glass gets 'dunked' in finely-chopped ice. Preparing a Campari is a real art: watch carefully how the barman does it!

The Duomo, Campari, Alfa Romeo and Pirelli are famed throughout the world. But what about La Scala, the world's most famous opera house? It, surely, is the true symbol of Milan. Approach it via the northern exit of the Galleria. On the way there, in the centre of the Galleria, you will pass the most famous restaurant in Milan, **Il Savini**. The cuisine in this highly traditional restaurant is superb, and the service excellent if slightly oppressive. Daytime customers should wear jackets and ties, and in the evening, dark suits.

Opposite is a culinary trauma: the former traditional restaurant of **Il Biffi** now houses a fast-food outlet. It really is a travesty that the city gave this place a licence – especially considering the fact that the Town Hall is only a few steps away, and that the Mayor himself is forced to witness this eyesore daily!

La Scala! And the magic of music, whether Verdi, Rossini, Puccini, Wagner, Toscanini or Karajan, Callas or Pavarotti. Sadly, the opera house closes for some time between 1998 and 2001. During the restoration work, the company transfers to another venue in the northeast of Milan. On your first visit it's best to get tickets for the cheap seats high up in the gallery *(loggione)*. It's here that you see the real music-lovers, the ones who arrive with scores tucked under their arms and know every note and every breath of the *primadonna* by heart. The opening of the opera season (7 December), by contrast, is a night of high glamour, when the wives of the city's rich financiers try to outdo one another with ever more elaborate gowns.

Take up your position at the foot of the statue of Leonardo da Vinci on the Piazza della Scala and admire the world's first ever opera house, built on the site of the former church of S Maria della Scala by Piermarini in 1777–8. Were it not for its contents the simple-looking facade would be easy to pass by. During a winter's day, I suggest you take a seat in the **Biffi Scala Toulà** and watch all the ballerinas and singers running by, wrapped up snugly in warm cashmere scarves for fear of catching cold. And in the evenings there is the elegant, yet all too human crush at the entrances to the building. The **Museo Teatrale alla Scala** (probably closed during the restoration period, but check locally) offers a rewarding look behind the scenes of this venerable institution.

To the right of La Scala is the elegant **Via Manzoni**, with its array of exclusive shops . But first there is one more museum you should visit, the **Museo Poldi-Pezzoli** (open daily 9.30am–12.30pm and 2.30–6pm; closed Monday), a treasure-trove of Milanese culture full of valuable paintings, porcelain and carpets.

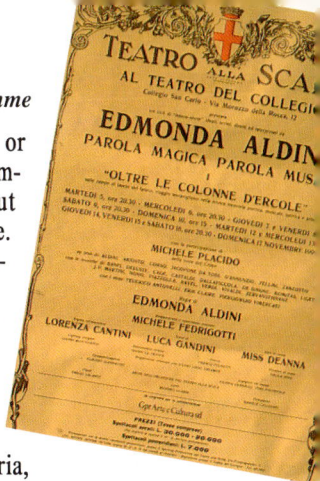

Your route continues along the Via Manzoni before turning left into the Via Romagnosi, a pretty little street with its sturdy and severely elegant *palazzi*. Now you are in the Via Monte di Pietà, which contains the Monte dei Pegni, a famous pawnbroker's shop visited by every social class, including society women. They transfer their fur coats here every summer, and the coats are carefully looked after in a refrigerator until the winter. This is useful because it keeps them out of the way, the pawn money comes in very handy, and after all, their husbands are sure to redeem the furs once the season begins again.

Now continue to the junction of the Via Verdi which will take you back to the Piazza della Scala, and from there follow the Via S Margherita, turning right into the Via Clerici to reach the **Palazzo Clerici**. This magnificent 18th-century Milanese patrician's house contains a real treasure: the banqueting hall known as the **Galleria degli Arezzi** with its fantastic barrel vault and its 119 sq. metres (1,280 sq. ft) of fresco by Giambattista Tiepolo – the Venetian painter's greatest work. The Palazzo today houses a study centre for international politics. Ask politely at the porter's lodge to be let in.

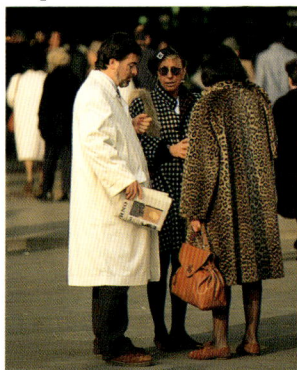

Milanese like to talk

You've reached the end of your stroll for today. From the Via Clerici it's a stone's throw to the Galleria again. How about a visit to Savini restaurant? Prices are far lower at lunchtime. You aren't wearing a jacket and tie? Then opt for **Biffi-Café** or the **Motta** self-service bar (top floor), both in the gallery.

In the evening you can visit **La Scala**, probably in its temporary home at La Bicocca, or go to a concert at the **Conservatorio** (Via Conservatorio 12, tel: 76001755). Or try a play at the **Teatro dell'Elfo** (Via Menotti 11, tel: 583158 96). Anyone keen on films can visit the following cinemas on the Corso Vittorio Emanuele II (behind the Piazza del Duomo): **Corso**, **Astra**, **Excelsior**, **Mignon**, **Arlecchino**. Wednesday's copy of *Corriere della Sera* will tell you what's on.

If you want to *fare bella figura*, elegant post-theatrical dining can be enjoyed at the **Biffi Scala Toulà** (100,000–200,000 lire a head) or in cosier surroundings at the **Caffè Milano** (Piazza Mirabello 1, open till 1am, closed Sundays), which serves good Irish coffee and delicious snacks at very reasonable prices.

The energetic can go dancing at **Beau Geste** (Piazza Velasca, not far from the Duomo), or head to a piano bar or club in the Brera or Navigli districts (see *Nightlife, page 70*).

For those who just feel like enjoying a good glass of wine, **Al Ronchi** (Via S Maurillo 7, not far from the Duomo) stays open very late.

DAY 2

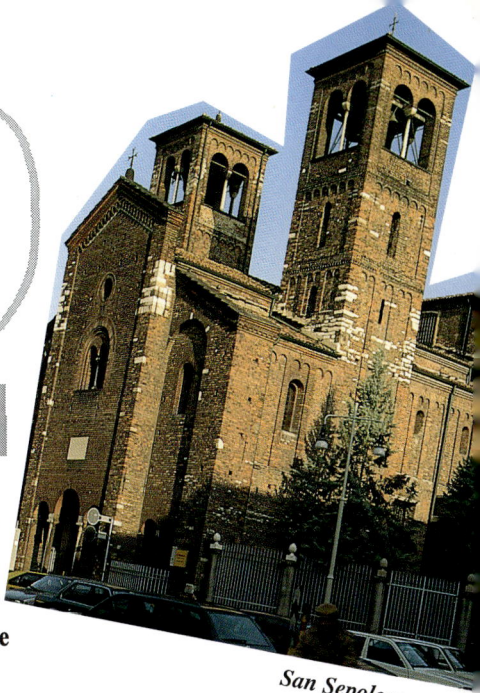
San Sepolcro

On the Trail of Leonardo da Vinci

From the Pinacoteca Ambrosiana to San Sepolcro, then to the Università Cattolica, the Museo della Scienza di Leonardo, S Maria delle Grazie, the Cenacolo di Leonardo and the Museo Archeologico.

– Tram 24 (Via Meravigli, Via Magenta); Bus 50, 54 (S Ambrogio); Taxi 'Pinacoteca Ambrosiana' –

Today you'll be making the acquaintance of some famous names from Milanese history: the Borromeo cardinals, Leonardo da Vinci and St Ambrose. This itinerary begins at the Duomo once again, from where you should follow the Via Orefici as far as the Via Cantù, into which you turn left to arrive at the **Ambrosiana** (Piazza Pio XI, tel: 86451436). The **Biblioteca Ambrosiana** (currently closed) contains over 30,000 books including the world's oldest book of miniatures and also Leonardo da Vinci's *Codex Atlanticus*, which comprises over 1,000 pages of drawings and sketches by the universal genius. In the **Pinacoteca Ambrosiana** (re-opens 1998) are works by Botticelli, Raphael, Titian and many other great painters – and in a glass case in Hall IV you'll find a lock of hair dyed blonde that once belonged to Lucrezia Borgia.

Leaving the Ambrosiana on the right-hand side via the Via Federico and passing several butcher's shops, you'll arrive at the **Piazza S Sepolcro**. Here, on the site of the former Roman forum, stands the church of S Sepolcro, consecrated to the holy sepulchre on the occasion of the First Crusade (open daily 8am–6pm). The Romanesque crypt of this church contains a sarcophagus with

Balcony of the Casa del Fascio, from which Mussolini made his speeches

reliquaries from the Holy Land dating from the High Middle Ages.

Opposite the church is a fine-looking Baroque building and a tower encased in cold, grey marble that Mussolini had added to the **Casa del Fascio** (1919) in 1939.

You can still find the original Milan in this area, with its narrow streets, craft workshops and elegant, patrician houses, most of them attractively restored. Off the beaten track and yet just a few steps from the Duomo, this is, however, one of the most expensive parts of the city (anyone buying property here has to expect a price equivalent to at least £5,000 per square metre). Walk down the Via Valpetrosa, then turn right down Via Torso and then right again straight away into the Via S Maurilio. At No 19 the wonderful courtyard of a 15th-century house awaits discovery – it is owned by the Crédit Agricole, Paris. In the Via S Marta you can admire the antique shops, and eat in the genuine rustic atmosphere of the **Trattoria Milanese** (tel: 86451991): the *risotti* are excellent, especially if accompanied by a glass of *Barbera*.

Afterwards, one of the finest Rococo houses in Milan is located at No 3, Via Nerino, along with its magnificent courtyard and tiny roof-garden. Back in the Via S Maurilio once more, follow it as far as the **Piazza Borromeo**, which contains the *palazzo* of the same name. An old Paduan family, the Borromeos had two particularly famous sons, the cardinals Federico and Carlo Borromeo, who were especially well-known for their charitable activities. Inside the *palazzo* is one of the most magnificent private courtyards in Milan.

Sometimes a friendly smile and a tip for the porter can open up finely-forged portals to reveal Milan's hidden treasures behind. Give this technique a try in the **Via Cappuccio**, where the *palazzo* at No 7 houses a magnificent cloister dating from the 15th century.

Now go right and then left into the Via S Valeria, which emerges behind the Basilica di S Ambrogio into the *piazza* of the same name. On the left you'll see the entrance to the **Catholic University** *(Università Cattolica)*, one of the best in Italy. The university, one of five in Milan, and housed inside a former monastery, was founded in 1921 on the initiative of Padre Agostino Gemelli. On the other side of this large and leafy square you'll see the entrance to the finest Romanesque church in all Lombardy: **S Ambrogio**. It is in this building, far more than in the Duomo, that the Milanese are made most aware of their history; the church was founded as early as the 4th century, when St Ambrose, patron saint of Milan, arrived here from Trier in order to take up the post of governor.

After having been elected Bishop, he placed himself at the head of the struggle against the Aryan heretics. It was Ambrose who invented the style of church singing known as Ambrosian chant; he persuaded the Emperor Theodosius to accept Christianity as the state religion, and he also won over Augustine, the great philosopher and future father of the church, to the Christian faith.

The church, flanked by two towers, is entered through its atmospheric four-door portal. The interior, with three naves, is simple and almost severe. On the right-hand side at the very back, in the dome of the small apse, there are some once gilded 4th-century mosaics as well as a picture of St Ambrose. The man himself was buried in the church in AD397, and the urn containing his bones is in the crypt beneath the high altar. Above the altar is the vast *Ciborium*, a colourful gilded baldachin or canopy. The heavily protected altar itself is completely covered with gold and silver containing around 400 precious stones – one of the most breathtaking pieces of religious art anywhere in the world. Ambrosian chant is still heard during the masses celebrated here.

Out in the square once more, note the pillar with the two holes in its base – they are supposed to have been put there by the horns of the devil.

The Festival of St Ambrose is celebrated every year on 7 December, and provides the cue for the *Fiera degli oh bei, oh bei* (a large fleamarket named after the calls of the stallholders) to begin on the Piazza. *La Scala* also begins its season on the same day. Anyone in Milan at this time should not miss paying a visit to this lively market. The children can fill themselves with *zucchero filato* (candy floss) or *calderoste* (hot chestnuts) while the grown-ups search for just the Christmas present they need at the various stalls.

Passing beneath the doors of the **Pusterla Gate** (which houses a remarkable museum of old weapons and instruments of torture) the itinerary now leaves the Piazza S Ambrogio and heads for the **Museo Nazionale della Scienza e della Tecnica di Leonardo da Vinci** in the Via S Vittore (open daily except Monday 9.30am–5pm; you

S Ambrogio, mother of Milan's churches

Leonardo da Vinci's 'The Last Supper'

can find a detailed description of this collection in the 'Pick and Mix' section of this book under 'Museums, Museums, Museums').

Having admired Leonardo's scientific somersaults, it's now time for his artistic ones. Turning left on leaving the museum, and then right after about 100 metres into the Via Zenale, you'll soon arrive in the Corso di Porta Magenta, and the *Cenacolo* (Refectory) of the church of **S Maria delle Grazie** (open daily except Monday 8am–2pm), where you can admire Leonardo's masterpiece *The Last Supper*. It's hard not to feel your heart beating just that little bit faster as you enter this former dining-hall of Dominican monks. The mural began to deteriorate soon after it was finished, due to the dampness of the wall, and the *tempera* technique used by Leonardo; subsequent attempts at restoration succeeded only in making matters worse. More skilful restoration techniques have been tried in recent years, but the mural's long-term survival remains in doubt. However, after 15 years' restoration, the work is finally visible to the public, although the area to the left of Christ is still unfinished.

The restoration incites controversy: admirers appreciate the authenticity of the result; detractors complain that the removal of tracts of paint has destroyed the narrative sense of the masterpiece. The painting, commissioned by Ludovico 'Il Moro' in 1495, displays several elements that were revolutionary at the time, for example the way the Apostles are depicted in realistically animated groups, with Judas included among them (fourth from the left). Miraculously, it survived an Allied bombing raid which almost completely destroyed the refectory which houses it in 1943. The church itself is the finest example of Early Renaissance architecture in Italy.

Continue along the Corso Magenta (anyone who feels like it can take a No 24 tram at this point to the Piazza Cordusio, where today's tour ends). After the junction with the Via Carducci you'll come face to face with the elegant **Palazzo Litta**, with its magnificent and typically Milanese golden-yellow Rococo facade. This *palazzo*, which was built by Ricchini, houses a fine little theatre at which I used to work many years ago. A short distance further on, at No 19, you could visit the **Museo Archeologico** (open daily except Monday 9.30am–5.30pm), but it might be a better idea to concentrate your remaining energies on the church of San Maurizio (open only on Wednesday, 9.30am–noon and 3–6pm, and on public holidays in summertime), with its fascinating frescoes by Bernardino Luini.

The Corso Magenta ends near San Maurizio, and the Via Meravigli begins, presenting a good opportunity for a break. The **Bar Cavour** on the corner has a pleasant atmosphere, and an *aperitivo con stuzzichini* (aperitif with canapés) is just the thing. The building next door contains one of the oldest *drogherie* (grocer's shops) in Milan; here you can buy genuine *zafferano* (saffron), needed to create the famous *risotto giallo* ('yellow risotto'). (See *pages 65–6* if you want the recipe.)

The **Libreria Milanese**, on the left, contains everything that has ever been written about Milan. And since you're now nearby, why don't you take a quick look at the **Milan Stock Exchange** (*Borsa*), Piazza degli Affari? A close-up view of the trading floor can be had from the small visitors' gallery: there they all are, the elegant managers clad in their grey flannel suits, the soul of Milan! And now, at the Piazza Cordusio, today's itinerary has come to an end. After you've taken the time to rest a bit back at your hotel, how about a visit to Giorgio Strehler's **Piccolo Teatro** (Via Rovello 2, tel: 72333222, closed Monday)? They may even be performing a popular favourite, Carlo Goldoni's *Servant of Two Masters* for example. Or how about a film? Cinemas **Centrale 1 and 2** (Via Torino 30) are good, as is **De Amicis** (Via de Amicis 1).

Or a literary coffee-house, perhaps? In the tiny **Caffé Portnoy** (Via de Amicis 1, open till 1am, closed Tuesday) you can spend an evening *à la Bohème* in the company of young poets and painters. Or there's always live music and all-night Latin American dancing at the **Sabor Tropical**, Via Molino delle Armi 18 (tel: 58313584).

The Navigli (canal quarter) makes a lively dining destination, with **La Scaletta** the natural choice for foodies in search of a great gastronomic experience. Alternatively, **El Brellin** is a folksy yet atmospheric spot for music-lovers (see *Eating Out* for details of both the above). There's a relaxed and cosy atmosphere in the unpretentious and good-value **Osteria del Nuoto** (Via Ascanio Sforza 105, on the Naviglio Pavese, open until late): wine, beer and simple, delicious food – including excellent home-made desserts – contribute to a convivial evening. The same goes for **Alzaia 26** (Alzaia Naviglio Grande 26), a gentrified *bistrot* nearby. Here one can dine on rabbit, cutlets or vegetarian dishes in the glassed-in courtyard. And to round the day off, one more romantic stroll along the Naviglio Grande before retiring to bed.

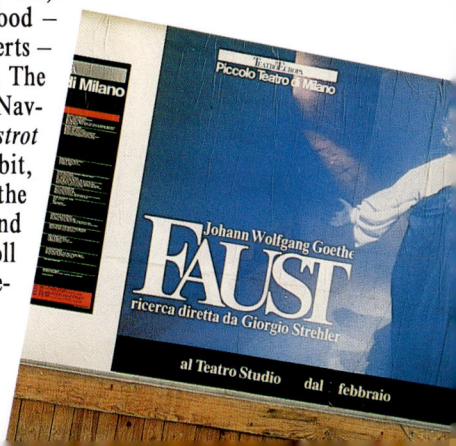

What's on at the Piccolo Teatro

The Castello Sforzesco, former seat of power of the Visconti and Sforza families

DAY ③

Renaissance Splendour

A journey from medieval Milan around the Piazza Mercanti to the Via Dante and then on to the Renaissance highlights of the Castello Sforzesco and the Torre del Parco; then to the Brera quarter of the city for a Bohemian end to the day.

– Metro M1 to Cordusio; Tram/Bus/Taxi 'Piazza Cordusio' –

The area between the Via Orefici and the Via Mercanti used to be the site of the *Comune di Milano*, or free city of Milan. The Middle Ages are still very much in evidence here, and on the **Piazza Mercanti**, former heart of the *Comune*, you can see the **Palazzo delle Ragione**, built in 1233, in which the City Council used to hold meetings until 1770. The magnificent **Loggia degli Osii** opposite, built in 1316, is, however, having to vie for attention with the ongoing restoration of the Piazza below.

Leaving the square via the Via Mercanti, you'll immediately arrive at the **Piazza Cordusio**, a centre of business and a major traffic junction. There are banks everywhere here, the Stock Exchange isn't far away, and buses, taxis, trams and Metro trains all stop here. If you now let your eye travel up the amazingly straight Via Dante you can't miss the massive Castello Sforzesco at the other end. Before taking a closer look at that, however, I suggest you first turn off about 50 metres further on into the Via Rovello, with the famous **Piccolo Teatro** at No 2.

Paolo Grassi and Giorgio Strehler founded Italy's first 'Teatro Sta-bile' here in 1947, and it later became world-famous. I always feel a little bit nostalgic whenever I pass by this particular spot: the 10 years that I spent in the drama department have had a marked effect on me.

Now go down a small street and return to the Via Dante, where you can enjoy an ice-cream in **La Cremerie** (closed Monday), the best *cremerie* in Milan (ice-cream shops are also referred to as *gelate-ria*). Further on, once you've arrived at the **Largo Cairoli**, with its Garibaldi equestrian statue, you'll have to pluck up some courage to cross the main traffic artery of the **Foro Buonaparte** in order to reach the Sforzas' castle. Napoleon, by the way, was crowned King of Italy in Milan's Duomo in 1805.

Assuming you're still safely in one piece once you've reached the other side of the street, you can now take a look at the **Castello Sforzesco**, which is the most important Renaissance structure in Milan. The castle was completely restored at the beginning of this century, and it was from here that the Visconti and later the Sforza dynasties ruled the city. The massive walls are 4m (13ft) thick, 31m (100ft) high and 200m (650ft) long; complete with its moats and drawbridges, the castle, situated right in the middle of the city, was impregnable, and formed the power base for the two families' dictatorial regimes.

The castle is entered via the mighty, upward-tapering tower known as the **Torre Filarete**, in fact a copy of the 15th-cen-tury original. Then, once you've crossed the inner court-yard, the Cortile delle Milizie, and passed through one more gate, turn right towards the **Musei del Castello** (daily ex-cept Monday 9.30am–5.30pm; more information on Milan's museums is contained in the 'Pick and Mix' section of this book under 'Museums, Muse-ums, Museums'). The various collections in the Castello in-clude paintings and sculpture but also arts, crafts and uten-sils. You can see a highlight in Hall 15: the not quite

The Arco della Pace

finished, magnificent *Pietà Rondanini* by Michelangelo, his last work before his death in 1564.

The Porta del Barco, on the other side of the castle, gives access to the **Parco Sempione**, 42 hectares (103 acres) of parkland in which the **Arco della Pace**, built in the monumental Milanese style of the 19th century, was erected in honour of Napoleon in 1807. Apart from this 'Arch of Peace', other sights include the **Palazzo dell'Arte**, with its fine art exhibitions, and the **Torre del Parco**, a tower over 100m (320ft) high, both constructed during the 1930s. Otherwise the park belongs to old people sitting on benches, groups of young people, or urban Indians practising their yoga. Unfortunately the park has to be patrolled by motorised *carabinieri* because it also seems to have become a popular battleground for skinheads and drug addicts. I suggest you only come here by day.

Artists Rino Sernaglia and Anna Canali

Having left the park along the Viale Gadio, where the tourist buses park, you'll pass by the **Acquario** in a Liberty palace (open daily except Monday 9.30am–5.30pm). This aquarium contains 48 pools with all manner of fish, reptiles and amphibians, and is a huge favourite with the city's schoolchildren.

If you now continue along the Foro Buonaparte for a while, you come to Teatro Studio (Via Rivoli 6) and the new Nuovo Piccolo Teatro. The Via Tivoli leads to the Via Mercato and Milan's Brera gallery area; many of the city's artists live in the courtyards of the simple houses here. (One of the leading lights of the artists here is Anna Canali, who runs the **Arte Struktura** gallery on the second floor of Via Mercato 1. Anna is the heart and soul of the group of artists known as Madi which includes such famous names as Rino Sernaglia, Salvator Presta and Dupré: the group is distinctive for its cinematographic, three-dimensional style.)

Art in Milan has a long tradition. The Romantic *scapigliati* artists of the last century (so named because they did not wear the tall hats fashionable at that time) turned the **Brera Quarter** into a real den of Bohemianism. In the Via Pontaccio, the extension of the Via Tivoli and the Via Fiori Chiari, there are rows of galleries and – as the Milanese call them – 'neoliberty' restaurants, where the patrons are very 'in' and very 'arty'.

Via Fiori Chiari

On the corner of the Via Solferino, Italy's important daily newspaper, the *Corriere della Sera*, provides political and intellectual fodder for those with Bohemian lifestyles in the Brera, many of them students from the Accademia delle Belle Arti, housed in the **Palazzo di Brera** on the Via Fiori Oscuri. Originally built in the 16th century for the Jesuits according to plans by Ricchini, the Palazzo also contains one of the most famous collections of paintings in the world: the **Pinacoteca di Brera** (open Tuesday to Saturday 9am–5.30pm, Sunday 9am–1pm).

In the Brera Quarter you can also visit the famous **Biblioteca Braidense**, the **Osservatorio Astronomico** and the **Orto Botanico** (all three of them are situated in the Palazzo di Brera, Via Brera 28). After such a *tour de force* you'll definitely be in need of some refreshment, which can be found at the already legendary **Bar Giamaica** (Via Brera 32, open till 2am, closed Sunday), a home from home for generations of painters, writers and musicians.

And this evening? *Che facciamo stasera?* Why not visit the **Nuovo Piccolo Teatro**, Via Rivoli 6, which you passed earlier. (Metro M1, get out at 'Lanzi'), where there's always a host of European avant-garde productions.

Cena dopo teatro? You can stay in the area for your post-theatre supper, and try out one of the many Chinese or Vietnamese restaurants in Milan's 'Chinatown': the restaurants in the Via Paolo Sarpi on the northern side of the Parco are cheap

Entrance to Castello Sforzesco

(30,000 lire a head) and usually stay open until 4am. If you didn't visit the above-mentioned Bar Giamaica this afternoon, you could always take a look at it this evening: half bar and half restaurant, this establishment is very lively and has imaginative dishes (main courses around 30,000 lire) and good cocktails created by the owner,

Elio Mainini. An alternative would be the candlelit **Rovello 18** nearby (Via Rovello 18, closed Sunday and Saturday lunchtime), the place to enjoy authentic Milanese cuisine in a cosy setting.

Want to hang out? The Brera is packed with trendy young bars and cafés, including **Orient Express**, Via Fiori Chiari 8, the latest fashionable spot for drinks plus live music.

PICK & MIX

1. In Search of Lost Milan

A short discovery trip into remote medieval corners around the Piazza Torino and Roman Milan: from the gourmet temple Peck to S Satiro, S Lorenzo and the Porta Ticinese, then on to S Eustorgio. The day ends in the Piazzale XXIV Maggio.

– Metro M1 or M3 to the 'Duomo' stop –

The following 'Pick and Mix' section provides itineraries that reveal several different aspects of Milan. As an interested observer, you can experience the city close up, beyond the familiar sights and views, or follow your own personal inclinations.

This itinerary begins at the Duomo, and explores the fascinating quarter south of the cathedral. The first stop is in the Via Torino, but even before beginning the route something may already tempt you to take a break: at No 9 Via Spadari (the first turning on the right along Via Torino) there's the enticing **Peck** (open 8.30am–7.30pm, closed Monday morning), a gourmet temple filled with superb aromas and tempting foods; step into the *rosticceria* and try out a few specialities. On the right are the *antipasti* with their delicious sauces, superbly arranged lobster, mouth-watering smoked salmon and seafood. Straight ahead of you is the cheese, the meat, the salami and the *pasta* – all of them super expensive, naturally.

Outside, in the Via Spadari, are more delicatessens belonging to the Peck family, such as the fishmongers and also the *Bottega del maiale*, the

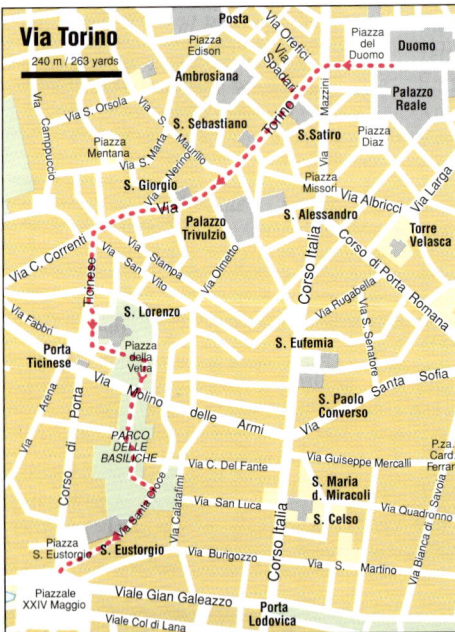

Via Torino

240 m / 263 yards

pork butcher's. In the nearby Via Hugo, Peck also own the gourmet **Peck Ristorante** and *enoteca* **Scoffone** – a wine merchant's premises where you can enjoy a quick aperitif and a small, utterly delicious snack to set you on your way.

Enough of food, for the time being – it's time for some culture. Back in the Via Torino, drop in on St Ambrose's brother: his church, **S Satiro**, was built in 1478 by Bramante, incorporating the former smaller Carolingian church. Don't miss the slender, magnificent baptistry on the right-hand side.

From there, return to the Via Torino and follow the street as far as **S Giorgio al Palazzo**, a rococo church with an interior adorned by *Scenes from the Passion of Christ,* a magnificent cycle of paintings by Bernardino Luini. The **Via Nerino** starts on the left-hand side of the church. In this street it is worth winning over the grumpy-looking doorkeepers of the medieval *palazzi* (a cheery smile and a small tip usually works), because there are some lovely gardens to be seen behind the gates. Also worthy of note in this respect are the Via San Maurilio (with its craft shops) and the Via S Marta.

After this diversion, continue along the Via Torino as far as the **Carrobio** (from the Latin word *quadrivium*, meaning road junction) where, keeping to the left-hand side of the street, you bear left and turn into the **Corso di Porta Ticinese**, with the true highlight of

Roman columns and the Basilica San Lorenzo

today's tour: the **Colonne Romane di San Lorenzo**. The Roman columns of S Lorenzo represent a magnificent period of the Roman and Early Christian history of Milan. Once part of a pagan temple, the columns were erected in the 4th century in the form of a triumphal entry arch in front of S Lorenzo – at a time when Milan was still the capital of the Western Roman Empire and the Emperor Constantine's Edict of Milan, which granted the Christians freedom of worship, had only just been passed. Times certainly do change.

In front of this, Milan's oldest basilica, stands a statue in memory of Constantine (the original stands in the courtyard of S Giovanni in Laterano in Rome), whose conversion in the year 312 led to the rise of Christianity as a world religion. Inside the basilica, the **Chapel of S Aquilino** was originally destined to be the mausoleum of the imperial family but was later linked to St Aquilinus, the 4th-century saint.

Having left S Lorenzo, you should take a swift look at the Porta Ticinese, one of the city's two surviving medieval gates. Rather than going through it, however, you should now make for the

S Eustorgio's striking campanile

Parco delle Basiliche behind San Lorenzo (beyond the Via Mulino delle Armi). Stroll along narrow, leafy paths, past mothers, nannies, old people, children and dogs, in a southerly direction until you reach the apse and the Romanesque church tower of the Basilica di S Eustorgio. The interior doesn't live up to the magnificent facade by any means.

The reliquaries of the Three Magi were kept here, in the Capella dei Magi, from the 4th century onwards until Barbarossa (Frederick I) took them to Cologne. Part of the reliquary was returned recently, and since then, on 6 January, during *Epifania* (Epiphany), a procession – complete with camels – leads from S Eustorgio to the Duomo. The Capella Portinari needs a mention, too: it's one of the finest pieces of Renaissance architecture in all Milan, with frescoes by Vincenzo Foppa.

Today's itinerary ends at the mighty Arco della Pace, on the Piazzale XXIV Maggio.

2. Around the Navigli by Bus

A round trip along the filled-in 'navigli'. Take the 97 bus (or the 96 bus going the other way) from the Piazzale Cadorna via Pusterla di S Ambrogio, S Maria presso S Celso, Basilica di S Nazaro, Università Statale, Palazzo Sormani and Corso Monforte to the Galleria d'Arte Moderna. Best done in the afternoon.

– Metro M1 to 'Cadorna'; or Taxi 'Piazzale Cadorna' –

Did you know that Milan was once a city of canals? That the city was filled with a whole series of them, mostly man-made, connecting it with the lakes to the north and the Po and Ticino rivers? That a system of sluices dating back to medieval times (Leonardo himself is said to have had a hand in their design) allowed ships to travel right into the heart of Milan? *Navigli* was the name given to these canals. The Milan so beloved of Heine and Stendhal contained a great deal more water than it does today.

During Emperor Barbarossa's time, the *navigli* were still defensive trenches that had been dug around the medieval city. In the 16th century they developed into important transport routes, and craftsmen, merchants and noblemen settled along them – just as they did along the Canale Grande in Venice. At the end of the last century the costs involved in their upkeep increased to such an extent that the *navigli* began to be filled in. The real *coup de grâce*, however, was delivered in the 1930s by the public transport system, which needed a great deal of space.

So just close your eyes and imagine for a moment that your bus is actually being 'rowed' around the city. The route begins *'alla Nord'* (at the **north station**) where to the left of the station, bus No 97 leaves from the Via Minghetti – or in the Piazzale Cadorna if you've arrived on the M1 Metro line. The route leads along the Via Carducci, past the Pusterla di S Ambrogio and through the Via De Amicis, both of which once formed part of the inner *naviglio*. Get off the bus after the Porta Ticinese at the **Parco delle Basiliche**.

In the Via Mulino delle Armi you could pay a quick visit to Guilia Cerronceva at No 7; her shop, **Il Gioiello di Pietra**, is a real treasure trove for those interested in fossils and minerals. You could also take a look at the church of **S Maria presso S Celso** to the right. A statue of the Madonna which is supposed to work miracles, situated next to the main altar here, is a popular destination for many Milanese newly-weds.

The journey continues on the 97 bus again, along the Via Santa Sofia, and is broken two stops further on at the junction with the Corsa di Porta Romana. Keeping to the left, you'll find yourself standing on the small square dominated by the **Basilica di S Nazaro**, which dates from the time of St Ambrose.

Behind the basilica, follow the small street that leads to the Largo Richini and the famous **Università Statale**, also referred to as *Cà Grande*, within its 15th-century walls. Inside the magnificent courtyard of the university, with its grandiose-looking Loggia, you can eat a sandwich and mix with the students, or take the Via Festa del Perdono back to the *naviglio*, which here is buried beneath the asphalt of the **Via Francesco Sforza** (named after the university's founder). Following this street as far as its junction with the Corso di Porta Vittoria, you'll come to the magnificent **Palazzo Sormani**. This glorious rococo building once stood on the bank of the *naviglio*, and today it houses the **Biblioteca Comunale** (open 9am–7pm). This well-stocked library also boasts an extensive collection of works by Stendhal.

Now cross the Corso and continue straight on until you arrive in the Via Visconti di Modrone. Stop here! It is time for a break in the **Taveggia** *pasticceria*, a bar and tearooms where lawyers from the nearby Palace of Justice go to gain strength between sittings; try the famous *budini di riso* (rice pudding), the delicious *panettone* (cake), *babà* (biscuits) and *meringhe* (meringues). By the way, the great Italian writer Alessandro Manzoni was born at No 17.

Students from the Università Statale

Back aboard the No 97 bus, get off two stops further on at the Corso Monforte. In the first street on the left, the Via Conservatorio, is the **Conservatorio**, founded in 1807 by Eugenio de Beauharnais, where Puccini once studied. Then comes the second-largest church in all Milan, **S Maria della Passione**, towering above the corner of the Via Bellini. The building was begun in the 16th century, and it contains Gaudenzio Ferrari's masterpiece, *Ultima Cena*. The chapter house, filled with frescoes, is also very impressive.

Back now to the Corso Monforte, where I suggest you take the bus once more and get off in the **Piazza Cavour**. From here, alongside the tall Palazzo dei Giornali, the bamboo-lined Via Palestro leads to the orange facade of the **Villa Reale**, housing the **Galleria d'Arte Moderna** (open 9.30am–5.30pm). This neoclassical building, designed by the Viennese architect Pollock, in which Napoleon once resided, displays 19th- and 20th-century painting and sculpture.

But now it's time for a good lunch or supper. How about **Leonardo's**, Via Senato 43, where you can end this tour *in bellezza* dining on *carpaccio, bresaole* and *filetti*.

3. Milan's Amsterdam

Walks (in the daytime) and entertainment (at night) along the 'navigli' canals at the Porta Ticinese. From the Piazzale XXIV Maggio via the Darsena to the Naviglio Grande, the Naviglio Pavese and the Corso San Gottardo.

– Tram No 15 from the Duomo to the Piazza XXIV Maggio or M2 to Porta Genova –

This route should really be done twice: by day in order to discover popular, everyday Milan, and then once again in the evening when the Milan 'scene' is in full swing – around the *navigli* is where the Milanese let their hair down and indulge in eating, drinking and dancing.

It's hard to imagine today, but as recently as the 1970s Milan had the third largest port in all of Italy in terms of tonnage, and barges carrying sand and gravel used to travel into the city along the *navigli*. Those days are gone now, but a look at the canals which survive is still very worthwhile.

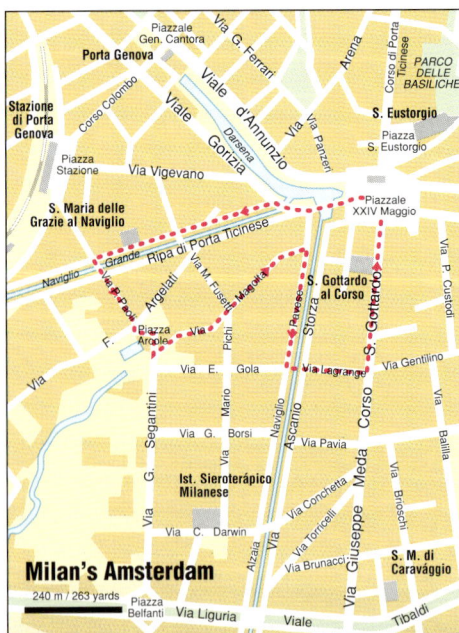

Milan's Amsterdam
240 m / 263 yards

From the Piazzale XXIV Maggio go up to the **Darsena** (the former harbour basin), taking a quick look at the lively **Mercato Comunale** on the way. The best view of the *navigli* and the old houses along their banks can be had from the green kiosk. On the other side of the Darsena the Fiera di Sinigallia, a flea market, is held on Saturday.

Down at the **Naviglio Grande**, all of Milan meets up on the last Sunday in every month to stroll around the **Mercatone dell'Antiquariato**. You can find objects of all shapes and sizes on the many

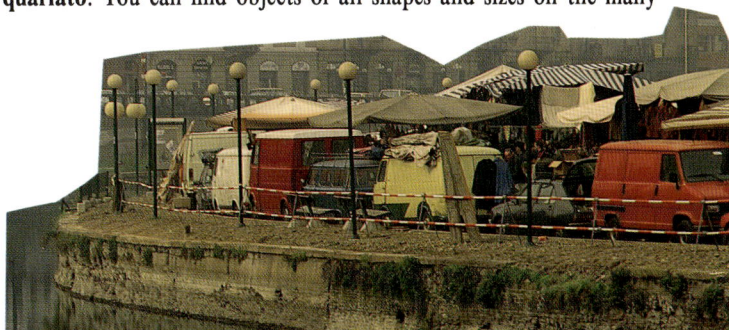

Sinigallia flea market

stalls here, some old, some not so old, and several of them priced astronomically high – but the atmosphere of the place is unique.

Walk along the right bank of the Naviglio Grande and after 100 metres or so you'll come across the remains of the **Vicolo dei Lavandai**, the old wash-houses that used to line the bank of the *naviglio*. The steps and stone slabs on which the women of the quarter washed their clothing – without detergent – can still be seen on the bank here. The Vicolo (alley) also contains the **El Brellin** restaurant and piano bar, by the way, which stays open late and serves excellent Milanese cuisine (closed Sunday).

Beyond the late 19th-century church of **S Maria delle Grazie** you can stand on the small bridge above the canal and observe all the small shops, art galleries and *pizzerie* along the bank. Just imagine, this artificial waterway was built in the 14th century, and it leads in a straight line all the way to the Ticino river, more than 50km (30 miles) away! If you were to turn right here and carry straight on you'd reach the **Stazione di Porta Genova**, a colourful working class quarter of the city, which incongruously boasts the gourmet restaurant of **La Scaletta** (see *Eating Out*).

For the time being however, leave the bridge on the left bank of the canal, the Ripa di Porta Ticinese, and turn immediately into the Via Paoli, following it as far as the **Piazza Arcole**. This is one of the rare areas of green in the quarter, and in the summer months you can swim in the **Piscina Argelati**, one of the nicest open-air pools in the city (open 10am–7pm). Afterwards turn left and enter the **Via Magolfa** where one of the city's remaining *osterie* with good *Barbera* wine, salami, sausages and sometimes even roast frog continues to keep the spirit of old Milanese hospitality alive.

The Via Magolfa opens out into the **Naviglio Pavese**, where the drinks are on me – after all, I live here! How about an aperitif mixed by my friend Carlo in the bar about 100 metres further on, on the right-hand side of the street? Or a *panino con birra* in the frenetic **Last Blast Birreria** near the beginning of the *naviglio*? By the way, note the large number of houseboats in the *naviglio*.

After a drink at Carlo's place you can cross the canal – no, a Canale Grande it definitely isn't, but it's still a canal: 33km (20 miles) long, and built by the Visconti. Over 1,400 barges used to travel along it each year. Following the **Via Ascanio Sforza** on the other side, you can sample the delicious, home-made pasta and risotto sauces at **Wilma e Riccardo** at No 17 (closes 8pm). At No 15 go through a connecting courtyard, with its fine old houses and balconies, and emerge on the other side in the Corso San Gottardo. Worthy of note here is the intimate little church of **S Gottardo al Corso** at No 6, with its designer windows. And now you're back in the Piazzale XXIV Maggio again, where you can take a No 15 tram back to the Duomo (Via Dogana side) or rejoin the metro at Piazza Genova.

Anyone who has a car with them should use it to visit the **Chiesa di S Cristoforo sul Naviglio** (a 10-minute car journey along the Naviglio Grande as far as Via S Cristoforo). Ludivico il Moro and Beatrice d'Este were married in this exquisite church, and it is still a favoured venue for Milan's prospective newly-weds.

And in the evening? *Follie!!* After 10pm the bars along the *navigli* are invaded, mostly by young people from the city centre and the drearier suburbs, all of them eager for a good time. In summer they sit along the banks and eat ice-cream, or patronise the houseboat pizzerias or listen to jazz at **Scimmie** (see *Nightlife*). This is the place to hang out. In summer, the 'N' navigli tram will take you back to the Duomo until 2am.

4. Around the City Walls

A trip along Milan's historic city limits on a No 29 tram (returning on a No 30). From the Piazza Missori to the Via Amadei, the Porta Romana, the Porta Venezia, the Giardini Pubblici with the Museo Scienze Naturali, and then on to the Piazza della Repubblica. Best done in the afternoon.

– Metro M1 or M2 to 'Duomo'
or Metro M3 to 'Missori' –

From the Duomo it's only 200m/220yds' walk south to reach the **Piazza Missori**, where today's discovery trip begins. On the way to the Corso Italia on the

The navigli district by night

Palazzo della Giustizia

Piazza Bertarelli, I suggest you take a small detour along the **Via Amedei**, one of the few streets in Milan to have retained its historic character – notice the beautiful inner courtyards glimped off the street as well as the excellent seafood restaurant **L'Assassino** (closed Monday).

On the Piazza Bertarelli, with the magnificent palace housing the **Touring Club** (Italian travel information available here), hop on a No 56 bus as far as the Porta Ludovica Viale. Continue on foot to Via Col di Lana, where you catch a No 29 tram for five stops to the Piazzale Medaglie d'Oro. Now you've reached the **Porta Romana**, erected in honour of the marriage of the Austrian archduchess Margaret to Philip III of Spain in 1599 (when Milan was Spanish). The gate once formed part of the Spanish walls, which extended for a distance of 11km (7 miles) around the city. To the left of the Porta Romana runs the Corso of the same name, a lively boulevard with theatres and clubs.

Take another 29 tram now and travel four stops on it to the **Porta Vittoria** in the Piazzale Cinque Giornati, so named because of the five-day-long rebellion in 1848 against Austrian rule. At the end of the Corso di Porta Vittoria, on the left hand side, you can't fail to see the colossal, almost Kafkaesque **Palazzo di Giustizia**, the scene of recent demonstrations in support of magistrate Di Pietro, a city hero. It's a real experience just wandering through the enormous halls inside this building; it makes you feel very small and very lost.

Mustn't get distracted, though! So take another No 29 tram now in the direction of the Stazione Centrale; after two stops it reaches the Piazza del Tricolore, and then two stops further on, the **Porta Venezia** (Piazza Oberdan). Just a few steps now in the direction of Corso di Porta Venezia is the entrance to the **Giardini Pubblici**. Laid out in Italian style with English elements, this park, 17ha (42 acres) in size, contains a 600-seat **Planetarium** (*Planetario*), which was founded in 1930 by Ulrich Hoepli, a Swiss editor of scientific books (open by appointment, tel: 29531181), and also the **Civico Museo di Storia Naturale**. The latter contains over a million insects, 100,000 fossils, 24,000 stuffed birds and 17,000 mineral specimens (open daily except Monday 9.30am–5.30pm).

Now you can get back by tram No 29 at the Porta Venezia (Piazza Oberdan), and continue in the direction of the Stazione Centrale for another two stops before saying a final farewell to the city's tram system at the **Piazza della Repubblica**. At the beginning of the Via Turati you will notice twin towers dating from the 1960s, while from the direction of the broad Via Vettor Pisani the Pirelli building, Milan's first-ever skyscraper, comes into view. The square also contains a number of luxury hotels, including the Principe di Savoia and the Palace (see *Hotels, page 88*).

Anyone feeling tired at this point may want to take the metro (line M3) back to the Duomo, otherwise it's onward, down the Via Turati, as far as the Piazza Cavour. On the way you pass Via Moscova containing the church of **S Angelo**.

This itinerary finishes at the Piazza Cavour, and with a clear conscience you can now take the M3 (Via Montenapoleone station) back to the Duomo, and go over to the Galleria for an aperitif at the **Camparino** (see *page 24*).

Outside a Milan gallery

5. The Art of Milan

A highly condensed tour of art galleries and antique shops.

– Metro M1 to the 'Palestro' stop and then on foot –

Got your city map? And your cheque book? And are your shoelaces tied? Good. On this trip you may be provided with an (aesthetic) offer you can't refuse: everything gets sold in Milan, and sometimes there are some really excellent bargains to be had.

As always, the tour begins at the Duomo, from where you take the M1 to **Palestro**. From here it's up to you!

Bergamini, Corso Venezia 16: an old-established gallery, 19th-century masters, held the first Masson exhibition in Italy.

Antichità Venezia, Corso Venezia 6: fine 18th-century paintings.

Galleria Blu, Via Senato 18 (tel: 76022404): founded 1957, contains works by international experimentalists such as Kandinsky, Klee, Léger, Turcato and Santomaso.

At this point you'll need to check the city map again so as not to lose your bearings:

Carlo Ariosto, Via Monte Napoleone 22: Italian paintings, precious objects and period furniture.

Agrifoglio, Via Monte Napoleone 21 (and Via Fiori Chiari): design and fashion.

Daverio, Via Monte Napoleone 6: De Chirico, Sironi, Savinio.

Arte Antica, Via Sant'Andrea 11: Pasquale Falanga has 18th-century French and Italian furniture, Italian, European and Chinese porcelain as well as Italian and German silver.

On now to the Via Gesù, doubtless the most renowned (ie 'in') gallery street of Milan:

Studio 111, Via Gesù 7: Vittoria Marinetti, daughter of the founder of Futurism, puts on select exhibitions.

Gilli, Via Gesù 17: a small salon, exhibitions of old art, especially 16th-century drawings and sketches; with luck you can find rare works by Tiepolo, Guercino or Luca Giordano. The gallery **Stanza del Borgo**, Via Puccini 5 (tel: 878360), is its opposite number.

Gian Ferrari, Via Gesù 19 (and Via Brera 30): one of the best-known galleries in Milan, founded in 1936, run by Claudia Ferrari who, like her father before her, is an art critic and an expert on 20th-century art; Sironi, Casorati, Martini, De Pisis, Pirandello, Rossi, etc. Large, richly-stocked warehouse and archive, with access allowed.

A gallery owner and his art

You've now reached the **Via Manzoni**, the cultural watershed between the area around the Via Montenapoleone (Milan's *rive droite*) and the Brera (its *rive gauche*).

Naviglio, Via Manzoni 45 (tel: 6551538), belongs to the Cardazzo brothers, pioneers of the international avantgarde in Italy; they were the first to introduce Pollock, Calder and Fontana to Italy.

Milione, Via Bigli 19: a side-street off the Via Manzoni, old-established gallery that introduced Léger and Kandinsky; various attractions ranging from Fellini sketches to Magritte.

Now it's time to take a look at the *rive gauche*, the **Brera**. After taking the Via Verdi past the Scala, follow the Via Brera, which was the centre of the gallery scene until the arrival of banks and financial holdings resulted in astronomic increases in rents.

Arte Centro, Via Brera 11 (tel: 86462213): classic abstracts by Prampolini, Cioni, Jiro Sugewana.

On the Piazza del Carmine not far from the Brera there are two more famous galleries:

Compagnia del Disegno, Via del Carmine 11: Alain Toubas and his friends have a collection of contemporary art here including work by Crocchi, Daminao and Keimitzuchi.

This beautiful little square with its cobblestones also contains the Lombard neo-Gothic church of **S Maria del Carmine** (containing a collection of fine paintings by Procaccini) and alongside it, next to a shop that sells delicious cakes and jams, is the **Braidense** gallery.

You'll probably have had enough gallery-browsing by now. But Milan does have an enormous number of art galleries, and anyone who isn't too tired can try one the following (probably not on the same day as the museums, though):

Gastaldelli, Piazza Castello 22 (not far from the Castello Sforzesco, tel: 863867): an Italian potpourri with Dorati, Scanavino, Sernaglia, Arroyo, Matta, Masson, Rainer, Tapiés.

Art 92, Via Moneta (metro: Cordusio): Miró, Picasso and a variety of watercolours.

Carla Sozzani, Corso Como 10 (tel: 653531): exhibitions, including major photographic retrospectives.

Yes, but what about the **antique shops**, you may be asking. These are scattered all over the city, but I recommend the area between the Via Torino, the Via S Maurilio and the Via Santa Marta, and also the vicinity of the Porta Ticinese (for less pricey shops). Here are a few specific recommendations:

Parronchi, Via Turati 6 (tel: 29006192): major Tuscan Post-Impressionist paintings.

Le Antiquarie, Via Fiori Chiari (tel: 86461730): old doors and wooden *objets d'art*.

Centro della Cornice, Via Lecco 15 (tel: 29531397): Tuscan and Venetian picture frames.

Carlo Teardo, Via Turati 6: antique silver, ivory and icons.

Silvia Blanchaert, Via Nirone 19: very attractive shop specialising in magnificent lamps (Murano glass by Venini) from the 1930s.

Longari, Via Bigli 15 (tel: 794287): rare and very valuable pieces from medieval sculpture to Renaissance tapestries.

To finish off, just a reminder of where and when to find Milan's best antique markets:

Oh bei, Oh bei on 7 December in front of S Ambrogio; **Fiera di Sinigalla**, held every Saturday on the Darsena del Naviglio (this is especially popular with architects and interior designers); **Mercatino di Brera**, held every third Saturday in the month; and the **Mercatino dell'Antiquariato** along the *navigli*, which is held on the last Sunday in the month.

Della Francesca,
'Madonna del Duca Federico'

6. Museums, Museums, Museums

A round-up of the city's best museums.

This selection really needs to be organised according to what you're interested in. You've already seen a few of Milan's 50 or more museums, and here is a more detailed summary. Each museum has useful catalogues; most are closed on Monday.

In the city of Leonardo, the first museum on the list is of course the **Museo Nazionale della Scienza e della Tecnica**: Via S Vittore 19/21 (open daily except Monday 9.30am–5pm; Metro M2 or bus Nos 50, 54, 96, 97; admission free). In the *Galleria di Leonardo* models based on Leonardo's original sketches can be

Raffaello Sanzio: 'Betrothal of the Virgin'

seen. There are also sections on aviation, transport, electricity, industrial machinery, motors, computer science, etc. The **Museo Navale Didattico** (open 9.30am–5pm, closed Monday; admission charge) next door has an interesting display of model ships.

The **Musei del Castello Sforzesco** (comprising the Museo d'Arte Antica and the Pinacoteca) are justly renowned (open daily except Monday 9.30am–5.30pm; Metro M1/2 to Cairoli or Cadorna; admission free). Antique arts and crafts: Michelangelo's *Pietà Rondanini* is in Hall 15; in Hall 3 there is the imposing equestrian statue of *Bernabò Visconti di Bonino*; the **picture gallery** contains works by Tintoretto, Mantegna and Bellini; the **Bertarelli stamp collection** has over a million exhibits, some of them priceless; the **archaeological and numismatic collection** contains prehistoric, Egyptian and other finds; and the **arts and crafts collection** has furniture, wall-hangings and ceramics.

Galleria d'Arte Moderna, Via Palestro 16 (open daily except Tuesday 9.30am–5.30pm; Metro M1, get off at Palestro; admission free). Italian and European painters, Futurists, Marino Marini Museum, French Impressionists, Renoir, Van Gogh, Cézanne.

Pinacoteca di Brera, Via Brera 28 (open Monday to Saturday 9am–5.30pm, Sunday 9am–1pm; bus No 43; Metro Lanza; tram Nos 1, 4, 8, 12 Piazza della Scala; admission charge). Because of a long-drawn-out argument between museum attendants and the museum administration a number of the best rooms may be closed due to *mancanza di personale*, under-staffing. The Pinacoteca, along with the Uffizi in Florence, is among the most important museums in the world and includes works by Piero della Francesca, Raphael, Caravaggio, Titian and Bellini as well as local Lombard masterpieces.

Museo-Poldi Pezzoli, Via Morone 8 (open by appointment only, tel: 794-889, daily except Monday 9.30am–12.30pm, 2.30–6pm, and Sunday 9.30am–12.30pm; the museum is two minutes' walk from the Piazza della Scala; admission). Botticelli; a wonderful picture by Pollaiolo, the 15th-century *Ritratto di giovane donna* (profile of a young woman); tapestries, hangings, clocks, weapons and more.

Museo Archeologico, Corso Magenta 15 (open daily except Monday 9.30am–5.30pm; bus Nos 50, 54, 96, 97; tram Nos 19, 24; admission free). Also interesting for Milanese history, with an impressive model of Roman Milan; also Prehistoric, Etruscan, Egyptian collections, etc.

Pinacoteca Ambrosiana, Piazza Pio XI, not far from the Duomo (re-opens in 1998). Founded by Federico Borromeo. Art by Botticelli, Titian and Raphael, plus Caravaggio's grandiose *Canestro di Frutta*.

Museo Bagatti Valsecchi, Via Santo Spirito 10 (open 1–5pm, closed Monday, admission free). A gracious palazzo housing Lombard and Italian works of art and Renaissance furnishings.

Alfa Romeo and Milan share the same coat of arms

Museo Storico Alfa Romeo, in Arese (9am–noon and 2.30–4.30pm; admission fee, but free on public holidays). See the prototypes driven by Nuvolari, Farina and Gangio (1950–55).

Museo Teatrale alla Scala, Piazza della Scala (fate uncertain between 1998 and 2001 – *see page 25*). Musical instruments, scores, letters, sculptures and photographs of operatic luminaries. A superb documentation of La Scala up to the present day.

Museo del Giocattolo e del Bambino, Ripa Ticinese 27 (open daily except Monday 9.30am–12.30pm and 3–7.30pm; admission charge; tram Nos 9, 29, 15, 30, Piazza XXIV Maggio). Toys through the ages.

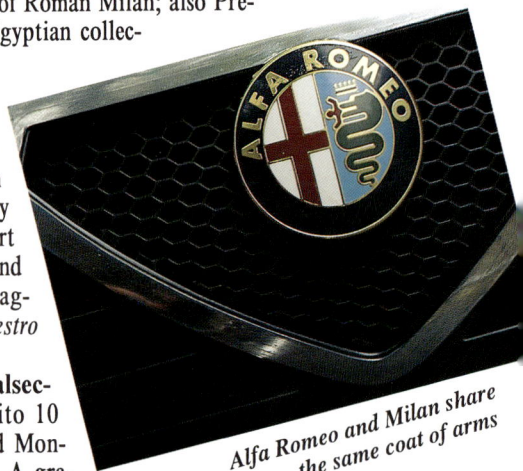

7. The Fashion World

A walk through the city's fashion quarter and its pedestrian precinct. From the Piazza del Duomo to the Corso Vittorio Emanuele II, S Fedele, the Via Manzoni, the Via Montenapoleone, the Piazza Babila and the Via Durini to the Largo Augusto. (Also see *Shopping* pages 77–81.)

Today is definitely the day to *fare una bella figura*. Today you can kit yourself out at Armani or Prada, put on some Ferragamo shoes, stick a Vuitton handbag under your arm and complete the entire outfit with a few pieces of Renaissance jewellery by Buccellati; for today you're off to the fashion sanctuary known as the *'quadrilatero',* where the ultimate in luxury can be admired – and even bought, if you have the cash. Do allow me, though, to point out the odd sight along the way too.

After visiting the Milanese super-boutique **La Rinascente** (which has a superb view of the Duomo, from the café and chic restaurant terrace on the 7th floor) you can start off at the top of the **Corso Vittorio Emanuele II** and turn left across the Via S Paolo and the Via Hoepli to reach the magnificent **Chiesa di S Fedele**. Built by the Jesuits in the 16th century, this is the equivalent of the Madeleine in Paris, and the temple of the Milanese aristocracy (magnificent choir stalls, exquisite confessional).

From here the route follows the Via Omenoni as far as the **Piazza Belgioioso**, home to Boeucc, a fine Milanese restaurant. On the corner of the Via Morone is a small brick *palazzo*, once the home of Alessandro Manzoni, Italy's greatest 19th-century author. The **Museo Manzoni** inside (open Tuesday to Friday 9.30am–12.30pm, 2–4pm) contains several of Manzoni's documents and personal requisites. The **Via Manzoni**, one of the busiest streets in the city, leads off the square. Neoclassical *palazzi* such as the **Palazzo Borromeo d'Adda** (No 39–41), where Stendhal once resided, and also the **Grand Hotel de Milan**, where Giuseppe Verdi lived and died, give the Via Manzoni its authentic *carattere ottocentesco*. Just a little further on is one of Milan's finest streets, the **Via Bigli** (the poet Montale once lived in the **Palazzo Bigli-Ponti** at No 11; its inner courtyard contains several fine 16th-century frescoes).

The **Via Monte Napoleone** is the backbone of all the other fashion streets of S Spirito, Borgospesso, Gesù, S Andrea and della Spiga. The *'Montenapo',* as it is familiarly called, does of course contain such great names as Missoni, Ferragamo, Gucci, etc. but here you will also find such shops as Lorenzi (knives large and small), Venini (Murano glass) and Jesurum (Venetian lace). The *palazzo* with the magnificent inner courtyard in the Via Gesù belonged to the late Gianni Versace, whose boutique is in Via Montenapoleone (No 2). Back in the Via della Spiga it's *alta moda* again: with Dolce e Gabbana clothes, Borsalino hats, Bulgari watches, and Krizia at No 23.

Situated in the Via S Andrea, the **Palazzo Morando** at No 6 contains the fascinating **Museo di Milano** (open 10.30am–7pm). Also in the Via S Andrea are Armani (No 9), with Armani Donna (womenswear) and the cheaper

Fashion's shop-window

Buon appetito!

Emporio Armani boutique in Via Durini.
You will also pass Fendi, Hermes, Prada,
Chanel, Ferré and Moschino. Now continue on in the direction of the *Montenapo* but just before reaching it, turn
left into the Via Bagutta. Here, in the
famous **Ristorante Bagutta** (tel:
76000902), the most important prizes in
the Italian literary world are handed out
each year. Many photographs of famous
artists adorn the walls, and the food is excellent too. The Via Bagutta emerges into
the Piazza S Babila (with a handy city information office and a
video point presenting what's on in Milan), which you now cross
in order to enter the **Via Durini**. Here you'll see some magnificent
baroque *palazzi* dating from the Spanish period, especially the huge
Palazzo Durini at No 24. Arturo Toscanini, the famous conduc-
tor, used to live at No 20.

The Via Durini leads into the Largo Augusto, from where the
Via Verziere (once a fruit and vegetable market) runs towards the
Piazza S Stefano and the huge Romanesque basilica of the same
name, which contains a fine fresco by Sebastiano Ricci.

If you're hungry at the end of this itinerary, the picturesque
townhouses around the Piazza contain a great many unpretentious
and very pleasant small restaurants frequented by students from the
nearby Università Statale. They include **Lo Stregone** (No 8, home-
made ice cream, beer); **Pane e Focaccia** (No 10, pizza slices, *panzerotti*); **Rosticceria** (No 10, very good *tavola calda*: try the stuffed
mushrooms).

8. From the Central Station to S Siro

**High-rise Milan: a look at a few of Milan's 'giants': the Stazione
Centrale, the Pirelli Building, the Stazione Garibaldi, the Cimitero
Monumentale, the Fiera Campionaria and the sports facilities at
S Siro. This route is best done in the morning.**

– Transportation: car or Metro M1/M2 –

Today's tour is going to take in some of the busiest parts of Milan, and you'll soon realise why the city is the industrial capital of
Italy.

The first stop, the **Stazione Centrale** (Central Station), is quite
enormous: the facade of this huge building alone is 207m (680ft)
long, and it was designed in 'Pharaonic-Neobaroque' style by the
architect Stacchini in 1912 (construction work took until 1931 to
complete). Although no rail journeys are planned for today, the interior is still worth a quick look. The ticket offices are completely
dwarfed by their 42-m (140-ft) high facade, and in the upper part

of the station the shopping gallery contains the Tourist Information Office and post office. Also spectacular is the enormous glass and metal roof spanning the platforms.

Outside once more, in the Piazza Duca d'Aosta (which is currently being landscaped), you are confronted by another vertical view: the **Grattacielo Pirelli** (Pirelli Building). Status symbol of Milan in the 1960s and headquarters of the Pirelli administration, this 124-m (400-ft) high skyscraper today acts as an administration building for the region of Lombardy. Designed by Gio Ponti and shaped like a ship's prow, the building seems to be cutting upwards through the sky towards a more promising future.

For the rest of this route you must take the Metro, descending now to get an M2 train (*metropolitana* No 2, the so-called 'Green Line') in the direction of Romolo, and get out two stations further on at the **Stazione Garibaldi**. Here, too, a couple more Postmodernist skyscrapers will have you gazing skywards. This area is increasingly becoming an administrative centre, with the usual problem of rising rents forcing out its original inhabitants.

One place will remain unaffected by all that, though: the **Cimitero Monumentale** – and monumental it certainly is. This cemetery, situated at the end of the Via Ferrari, has a fascinating and highly morbid assortment of tombstones: Neo-Gothic, Neo-Byzantine, ultramodern and also some unbelievable, almost Hollywood-style, kitsch. Alessandro Manzoni and Carlo Cattaneo are among those to have found their final resting place here.

Leaving the cemetery, return to the Stazione Garibaldi. From there, take the M2 once again in the direction of Romolo, and then change at **Cadorna** to the M1 in the direction of Molino Dorino, getting out at the stop called **Amendola Fiera**.

If a trade fair is taking place – and it's highly likely because the **Fiera Campionaria** is one of the most important trade fair centres in Europe – you should definitely take a look inside the exhibition buildings, where 10,000 firms vie for the attention of 5 million visitors every year.

Or otherwise you can follow the boulevard-like Via Monte Rosa with its townhouses in a southeasterly direction until you reach the **Piazza Buonarotti**, its centre adorned by a statue of Giuseppe Verdi. At No 9 on this Piazza is the famous building founded by Verdi in 1899 known as the **Casa di Riposo Giuseppe Verdi**, a happy home for retired musicians who, as the composer put it, were "less lucky than I". The tomb of the great man and his wife, Giuseppina Strepponi, can be seen in the funeral chapel in the grounds (ask for permission at the porter's lodge first!). Many great

Stazione Centrale

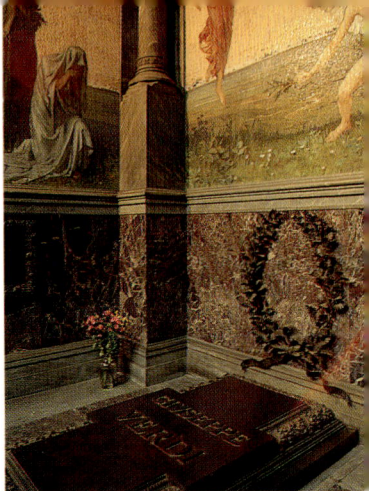

The tomb of Giuseppe Verdi

artists visit the Casa Verdi and the concerts held in this retirement home, which really is a happy one, have become famous.

Continue onwards on the M1 (the Metro entrance is right next to the Casa Verdi) in the direction of Molino Dorino until you reach the **Piazzale Lotto** (2 stops). You are now in the wonderful **Quartiere di S Siro** where not only the largest sporting facilities in the city, but also the magnificent villas and huge gardens belonging to the super rich Milanese are to be found.

Follow the Viale Caprilli and you'll arrive right at the **Stadia Meazza** (Stadium), in which Milan's two famous football teams, Inter Milan and AC Milan, play their matches (I support AC Milan). Football fans may tour the stadium (tel: 48707123 to book) while others may prefer a walk in the nearby **Parco di Trenno**.

Back in the Metro at the Piazzale Lotto, get out two stations further on in **Lampugnano**, where you'll be met by something really rather remarkable: a mountain in Milan. Well, not quite, but the **Monte Stella**'s still a good 170m (550ft) high: it was built from the rubble left behind by World War II. Over the years it's become rather a nice park, and the Milanese even ski down its slopes in the wintertime – a snow-cannon provides the necessary slippery surface. The famous **Palatrussardi** (tel: 33400551), venue of Milan's biggest rock concerts, is also close by here. So, if you're planning to come this way again, don't forget your skis or your concert ticket!

9. Milan's Parks

Off for some fresh air! A jogging and walking tour through Milan's new parks: Forlanini, Azzurro, Zoo Preistorico.

– By car and on foot; distance: 60km (37 miles); duration: 1 day –

Today it's out into the wild green yonder away from the typical 'Milanese air'.

I should start off by mentioning that you can find several areas of green in the heart of the city, some of them created only recently, and you've actually seen some of them already: there's the **Parco Sempione**, the largest of the city's parks; the **Parco Ravizza**, not far from the elite Università Bocconì; the **Parco Lambro** on the Lambro river to the northeast, with its artificial hills; the **Parco Solari** with its ultra-modern indoor swimming pool (open in winter only); and last but not least, the park surrounding the **Villa Litta** to the northwest of the city.

The most important areas of green, the so-called *giardini*, are of course the **Giardini Pubblici** and those at the **Villa Comunale** with its famous planetarium. There is also the **Orto Botanico** in Brera and the **Giardino Guastalla** near the *Policlinico* in the Via Francesco Sforza. The **Parco di Trenno** was laid out quite recently in the S Siro area, and another fine place is the **Parco della Villa Reale** in Monza (a recommended stopover on a trip to Monza, the Brianza and Lake Como).

Today involves a bit of park-hopping, but it shouldn't be too exhausting because all the destinations are situated in the same area of the map, bounded by Forlanini, the airport at Linate, the Idroscalo lake, and the Adda river. Take a jogging outfit and some running shoes, and for those travellers with a roof-rack, possibly a mountain bike as well.

If you're coming from the centre and the Piazza del Duomo it's best if you start off from the Corso Porta Vittoria. First you need to drive along the Corso XXII Marzo, then take the Viale Corsica and then the Viale Forlanini, after which you go under the Tangenziale Est, and *voilà* – you've arrived at the **Parco Forlanini** on the left. The Parco Forlanini encompasses 75,000 sq metres (18 acres) of meadow and forest, concealing several interesting and typical Lombard farms (known as *cascine*). Two of them are due to provide space for the new Botanical Garden: the **cascina Villa Landa** (Via Corelli 142) and the **cascina Case Nuove** (Via Corelli 124). Then there's the new all-purpose SAINI sports centre (tel: 7561280) with its 150,000 sq metres (36 acres) providing more than enough room for almost any land-based sport you care to think of.

If you would rather spend your time relaxing near water, you should continue along the Via Forlanini, behind the park, to the **Idroscalo**, a 700,000 sq-metre (170-acre) artificial lake. The neighbouring park, the **Parco Azzurro**, named after the colour of the lake, is the setting for all kinds of summer events. It's also the place to find a little forest clearing or a sunny meadow and unpack a picnic. Health freaks saddle up their bicycles, speedsters head off for the Go-Kart track and swimmers stay next to the lake, where they can also take boat rides. The lake itself measures 2,500m (8,200ft) long and up to 400m (1,200ft) wide, and the water is up to 4m (20ft) deep; motorboat and rowing races are held here, and in the summer the banks are crowded. If you don't fancy sunbathing, boating or water-skiing, you can always hire a seaplane!

Back to the car now, and continue in the direction of Melzo along the Strade Rivoltana, which connects

In the Parco della Villa Reale

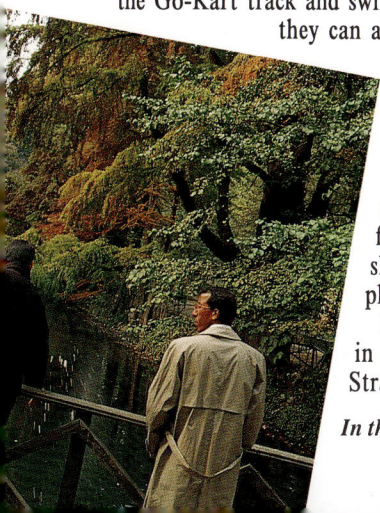

Segrate, Milan and San Felice. **Rivolta d'Adda** is 15km (9 miles) further on. As you can probably tell from its name, this town is built alongside the 313-km (195-mile) long River Adda, the grassy banks of which form one enormous conservation area. Not far from its source the river flows through the Parco Nazionale dello Stelvio, and here through **Parco dell'Adda**.The attractive main square of Rivolta is definitely worth a short stop, as is the 11th-century **Basilica di S Maria e Sigismondo** with its mighty apse and proud-looking campanile.

Percorso Vita

10

Saltellare in avanti alternativamente a sinistra e a destra sopra il tronco con i piedi uniti.

5x 10x

Keep fit!

To the southwest of the town, on the left bank of the Adda, is the **Parco Zoo della Preistoria** (open March to November, 9am–sunset; admission charge). A 4-km (2.5-mile) long path here runs through forest that is jungle-like in places and, to the delight of children (and their parents), not only leads past compounds containing living animals but also lifelike scale models of dinosaurs (you'll be amazed just how large they actually were), prehistoric human settlements, cavemen, etc.

If you're feeling ready to enjoy some good food at this point, try the specialities served at the **Trattoria al Capanno**: snails, venison, pork, mushrooms, and many other delicacies. The tourist menu is very reasonable, and very filling too (tel: 0363/78024; restaurant closed on Tuesday). And this is where your excursion into the countryside comes to an end. Now it's back to the stress of the big city; I hope you'll avoid the worst of the rush hour back.

10. Milan of the Future

In search of the city of the future in the area around Milan: from Segrate to Milano 2 and Milano 3 and then on to Milano Fiori, plus a detour to Cascia Vione.

– Travel by car; distance 70km (40 miles); best done in the afternoon (less traffic). Take a map and compass! –

Today's itinerary will introduce you to some of the new and ever-expanding outlying districts of Milan. The creation of the new suburbs became embroiled in the corruption scandals of the 'Tangentopoli' *(see page 15)* so further expansion has come to a standstill.

The route starts in the Piazza del Duomo from where you travel in the direction of Linate, via the Corso Porta Vittoria, Piazza XXV Giornate, Corso XXII Marzo and the Viale Corsica as far as the 'Tre Ponti', or 'three-bridge' underpass which leads under the railway (the Via Piranesi, which runs parallel, contains Italy's first ever ice rink, built in 1923). Now

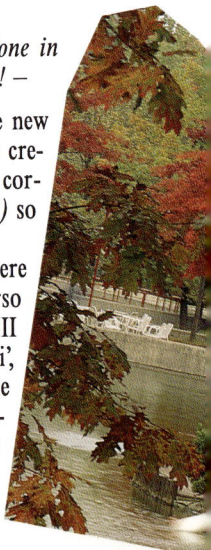

Super-modern living

turn into the Viale Forlanini, cross beneath the Tangenziale Est, which you'll be taking on your way back, then over the polluted Lambro river, along the side of the Parco Forlanini *(see 'Milan's Parks')* until you finally end up at the airport area of **Linate**.

The Viale splits into two here, and you should take the left lane signposted to **Rivoltana**, and then drive along the previously mentioned Idroscalo Lake. Straight after the Idroscalo you'll reach the municipality of **Segrate**, the location of three company buildings that can pride themselves on having what is perhaps the most expressive modern industrial architecture anywhere.

The most impressive is the building belonging to the **Mondadori** publishing house. Designed by architect Oscar Niemeyer and built in 1974, this building is a colossal edifice made up of three sections, with the supporting part made of reinforced concrete and with snow-white arcades propping up the upper storeys with their offices; down in front of the building there is a friendly little lake with swans and ducks. To the right and to the left are the buildings belonging to the firms **3M** (designed by Pestalozza) and **IBM** (designed by Zanuso), both of them glass, steel and cement structures built in 1977.

Not far away from the tiny lake of Malaspina is **Milano S Felice**, the city's first purely residential suburb and also the first ever *città giardino* (garden city) in Italy (architects: Magistretti and Dominioni), with its own shopping centre and its terraced houses surrounded by parkland which are actually quite expensive to buy. Further north and not very far from the Lambro river is **Milano 2**, another spacious and elegant residential area with its own pedestrian precincts: it's a mixture of private residence construction (Fininvest, Berlusconi's giant holding company) and shopping centres, and over 10,000 people have made their homes here. The control centre of media mogul and ex-Premier Silvio Berlusconi's **Canale 5**, the best-known private TV station in Italy, is also located here.

Now travel back down the Strada Rivoltana and take the Tangenziale in the direction of Bologna. At the S Giuliano junction, where the A1 begins, you should continue along the Tangenziale (which has now become the Tangenziale Ovest, i.e. west) and take the turn-off marked Naviglio Pavese to join the Strada Statale 35. Keep to the left (SS 35 dei Giovi) in the direction of

55

A hungry future generation

Binasco Pavia, following the 33-km (20-mile) long Naviglio Pavese that flows from Milan to Pavia; in former times it used to be an important transport route, and also provided irrigation for the fields. After a few kilometres, turn off left to Rozzano and then travel on to Basiglio.

This is the location of **Milano 3**, the most recent of the residential areas that were built during the 1980s and 90s: another 10,000 people live here, occupying a surface area of 1,700,000 sq metres (420 acres). This area is self-sufficient too, with its own shopping centre and several schools, and a commuter bus plying to and from the city centre (buses leave every 20 minutes). Not everyone can afford to live here, however, especially at prices of around £2,000 per sq metre (10.7 sq ft) of living space. Nevertheless, the whole place has a melancholy atmosphere – it's a ghetto of the wealthy with countless orange-coloured prefab terraced houses. In the evenings (the only time of day when the majority of its hardworking inhabitants have any free time) the compulsory swans in the compulsory lake are subjected to compulsory contemplation before the lights get switched off.

Close by is the **Cascina Vione**, the best-preserved 17th-century farm in the entire area, with Baroque archways, eight inner courtyards, its own chapel, a manor house and servants' quarters, stables and barns. Sixty families lived here until only very recently, supporting themselves by farming. Unfortunately the last of them will soon have to move out to make way for *nouveaux riches* and their dreams of 'doing up' country houses.

Returning to Rozzano, keep to the right in the direction of Milan. After a brief journey you will reach a fork in the road at which you should turn left in the direction of Milano Fiori-Assago. It won't be long before you arrive in the ultra-modern administrative area of **Milano Fiori**, conveniently situated between the Tangenziale Ovest and the A7 to Genoa, and probably the most futuristic modern services centre in the world. In these cleverly-designed buildings with their mirror glass facades, some 12,000 people work for around 200 different companies (mainly connected to computing, marketing, congress centres, etc.).

The **World Trade Centre** (architect: Renzo Piano) here is a sight worth seeing, as is the **Euromercato**, which occupies a surface area of 10,000 sq metres (107,000 sq ft). There's another enormous residential area in nearby Assago, with the gigantic **Palaforum**. But now why not take the motorway back to Milan and finish your trip into the postmodern era along the good old *navigli* (canal quarter), over a dish of ravioli or risotto, plus a nice glass of *Barolo* wine, in the Piedmontese **Ristorante Aurora** in the Via Savona? Good idea?

EXCURSIONS

11. Abbeys of the Bassa Milanese

A trip to three medieval abbeys to the south of Milan: Viboldone, Chiaravalle and Morimondo.

— By car; distance approximately 140km (90 miles) —

Today's excursion starts out at the Porta Romana in the direction of the Piazza Corvetto. Drive as far as the circular flower bed, where the Via Emilia, which was first laid out by the Romans, begins, and join the motorway that runs parallel, the Autostrada del Sole, a little later. On your left you'll pass the high green buildings of **Metanopoli**, one of the first satellite towns to be built after World War II.

At San Giuliano Milanese the route continues on to **Viboldone** with its abbey of the same name. It isn't a famous abbey, but is still quite enchanting architecturally; a late 12th-century red brick edifice with a unique Romanesque-Gothic facade, and a portal decorated with sculptures. The interior is adorned by simple 14th-century frescoes by Giusto De'Menabuoi, a talented pupil of Giotto (*The Last Judgement* above the main altar is especially striking).

Entering the Abbazia Viboldone

The abbey is the home of Benedictine nuns who run their own printing works and sell pictures of the church (visiting times 7am–12.30pm, 2.30–6.30pm). In the town itself there's very good value food to be had at the **Osteria del Ponte** (open all day every day except Saturday lunch) with its Lombard home cooking and delicious wine from the hills around Pavia.

Now go back to the nearby motorway, to S Giuliano or Sesto Ulteriano (by the way, be super-careful when studying the forest of road signs here: you need to take the Tangenziale Ovest in the direction of Pavia). Leave at the exit marked **Vigentina** and enter the road of the same name which then turns into the

57

Angel in the Abbazia Viboldone

Via Ripamonti. Then take the first road off to the right (yellow sign to Chiaravalle) and a few minutes later you'll arrive in front of the famous **Abbazia di Chiaravalle** (open 9am–noon and 2–5pm), founded by Bernard de Clairvaux and one of the largest Cistercian abbeys in Italy. The monks sell honey and delicious home-made spirits in the small shop here. The facade was redone in the 16th century but the fine transept floor is in need of restoration. The interior is predominantly late 12th-century, and the domed vault is decorated with fascinating frescoes by artists of the Giotto school. Also remarkable is the Madonna fresco by Luini (on the right hand side of the transept, at the top of a stairway) because of its *trompe l'oeil* effect, while the 14th-century campanile is particularly elegant.

Now travel back the same way you came (Tangenziale Est) and join the Autostrada dei Fiori Milano-Genova (A7), which you leave again at the second exit marked Bereguardo, following the direction of Motta Visconti/Vigevano. You're now in the **Parco Naturale di Ticino** conservation area: 90,000 hectares (220,000 acres) of officially protected fauna and flora, with groves of poplar and elm inhabited by herons, ducks and seagulls. If you feel like it you can leave the car at this point and take one of the many footpaths leading to the Ticino river, which flows right through the woods here. Should you be hungry, I strongly recommend the town of **Zelata**, situated 7km (4 miles) from the motorway: there you'll find a tiny *trattoria* with excellent home cooking, sandwiches and *Barbera* wine.

Finally you reach the grandiose **Abbazia di Morimondo**, which gets its name from its founders, Cistercian monks from Morimond in France. The abbey is a late 12th-century brick building with a simple facade and a huge rose window that bathes the interior, with its three naves and cross vault, in magnificent light on sunny days. The abbey is still inhabited by Benedictine monks, generations of whom cultivated the land around it and created the rice paddies that still exist today.

Leaving the abbey, take the left fork in the road at Ozzero to **Vigevano** (population 70,000, famous for its shoe production). Sights worth seeing here include the **Piazza Ducale**, a wonderfully harmonious square, built on the orders of Ludovico il Moro in 1494, surrounded by town houses above pillared arcades and providing a

view of the impressive facade of the town's 16th-century **Duomo** (the rarely open cathedral museum contains magnificent Flemish tapestries). The **castle**, built by Bramante, is undergoing restoration, with its 70-m (230-ft) high tower and its stables. At this point anyone who missed the last two opportunities to eat should adjourn to the excellent **Al Convento** three-star garden restaurant, Via del Convento 8 (closed Tuesday).

The route back to Milan follows the road along the Naviglio Grande, through Abbiategrasso, keeping to the canal all the time until the Porta Ticinese.

Facade of the monastery of Certosa di Pavia

12. Pavia

Pavia and its hills: its Carthusian monastery, the Oltrepò Pavese and the Valtidone. A trip into the the land of the Lombards, rounded off by some very nice wines from the Oltrepò Pavese.

– Ideally by car but also by train (30 minutes from Milan); distance 140km (90 miles); duration 1 day –

Today you'll be taking a trip back into the depths of the Middle Ages, when the Plain of the Po was conquered by hordes of tribes from Northern Europe. The people who stayed the longest were the Lombards, and Pavia was their capital city for over 200 years: so why not find out more about them!

Setting off from the Darsena, you should follow the Naviglio Pavese as far as Binasco, and 11km (7 miles) further on you'll come to the famous Carthusian monastery, **Certosa di Pavia**. Park the car first, and then walk over to the square in front of the breathtaking facade of this building. (Opening times: 9.30–11.30am, 2.30–4.30pm, and until 6pm in the summertime; closed Monday). The guided tours are provided by Cistercian monks, successors of the original Carthusians (the rest of the monks obey vows of silence).

Built at the behest of Gian Galeazzo Visconti in 1396 to provide a worthy site for his family vault, the Certosa is one of the foremost monuments of the Lombard Renaissance. Priceless works of art have been collected together here over the centuries. The 15th-century facade was left incomplete, true, but that hardly diminishes its effect.

The interior, half Gothic and half Renaissance, is decorated with numerous chapels and contains works by Bergognone and Perugino. Don't miss the choir in the presbytery and the ducal vault in the transept. The interior and the facade are by Amadeo. Leaving the right transept, the visitor will enter the **Small Cloister**, generously decorated with 15th-century terracotta figures, and then the **Large Cloister**, with the cells of the Carthusians ranged along its sides. Outside the refectory, directly in front of the abbey's defensive wall to the right, is a *cascina* dating from the 18th century which today contains a wine shop (wines from the Oltrepò Pavese).

But there's not only wine – traditional *Chartreuse* is for sale here too. What *is* it, exactly? A herbal liqueur, made by monks according to the (naturally secret) original medieval recipe from Grenoble, it comes in two forms: yellow and sweet *(Chartreuse jaune)* or green and dry *(Chartreuse verte)*. The *Gra Car* on the barrels stands for *'Gratiarum Chartusia'*.

Fill the car boot with your various purchases and drive on to **Pavia**. This town on the Ticino river (population 100,000) had its heyday between the 6th and 8th centuries when it was the proud capital of the Lombards, and it still contains several well-preserved reminders of that time. In the 14th century the Visconti arrived and gave this traditional university town its magnificent castle. Pavia's prosperity is due in no small measure to its agriculture as well as its clothing (especially fur) and furniture industries.

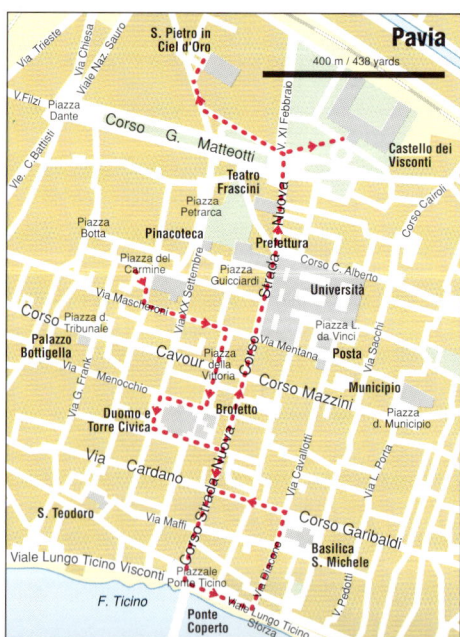
Pavia

Your stroll around town will take in the following: S **Michele, Duomo, Castello dei Visconti,** and S **Pietro in Ciel d'Oro.** The best place to leave the car is the Piazza del Carmine (see map), which gives access to the **Piazza della Vit-**

The Ponte Coperto in Pavia

toria, lined with 14th- and 15th-century houses and arcades. On one side, behind the Duomo, is the 12th-century **Broletto** (Town Hall), and next to the Duomo, the unsteady **Torre civica,** or 'municipal tower'. The **Duomo,** based on sketches by Amadeo, Leonardo and Bramante, is a fine example of the Lombard Renaissance style. Anyone who takes a look inside is sure to be impressed by the grand interior with its enormous *cupola,* and by the crypt, which was designed by Bramante.

Next continue into the Strada Nuova, which at one point provides a view over the Ticino promenade and the **Ponte Coperto** bridge. The Via Diacono on the left leads to the **Basilica S Michele,** founded by the Lombards and restored in the 12th century, and probably one of the finest surviving Romanesque structures anywhere in the world. Kings and emperors were crowned here. The facade, in three sections, contains numerous human figures and fantastic creatures (note the small *loggie* above the apse and the crossing tower). The interior is remarkable for its severe beauty: three naves, with pillars and galleries. The triple-aisled crypt, supported on columns, is another highlight.

Return from S Michele to the Strada Nuova and head back to the north until the 18th-century **Teatro Frascini,** designed by Bibbiena, soon appears on your left. To the right is the 11th-century **Università,** one of Europe's oldest and most respected, containing, in addition to its magnificent inner courtyards and arcades, a disused monastery. The neoclassical facade is by Piermarini and Pollock.

Three very well-preserved **Romanesque towers** can be seen on the nearby Piazza Leonardo da Vinci. And towering straight ahead is the square shape of the 14th-century **Castello dei Visconti.** The northern part was destroyed but then rebuilt after the famous Battle of Pavia in 1527. The castle contains the **Museo Civica e Pinacoteca** (Municipal Museum) with works by Bellini, Boltraffio and Correggio (open 10am–noon, 2.30–4pm).

From the Piazza Castello turn left along the Corso Matteotti, and then once you're on the same level as the bus station, turn right towards the Romanesque church of **S Pietro in Ciel d'Oro,**

Landscape near Albareto

consecrated in 1132. Inside this triple-naved church it's worth noting the presbytery above the crypt, and the Gothic **Arca di S Agostino** above the main altar, containing the mortal remains of St Augustine.

It's worth enjoying a heavy lunch in Pavia: the pricey **Locanda Vecchia** (Via C Riboldi, by the Duomo) serves tasty Lombard dishes. Return now to your car for a tour of the hilly area known as the **Oltrepò** (i.e. 'beyond the Po', as seen from the north) **Pavese**. The slopes here are crowded with vineyards and villages, and the good air means good (DOC) wine, which the vineyards bottle and sell themselves: *Bonarda, Barbera, Barbacarlo, Buttafuoco, Croatina* (red), and *Pinot, Cortese* and *Riesling* (white).

From Pavia it's also worth travelling via the towns of Castéggio, Broni and Stradella to **Castel S Giovanni** in Valtidone. The shops in the surrounding villages (Albareto, Vicomarino, Ziano Piacentino, Pianello) are stuffed full of delicacies just waiting to be discovered: *agnolotti ripieni* (a kind of ravioli with cheese filling), *tortelli* (filled with Ricotta cheese or spinach), *panzerotti* (ravioli with fresh cheese), a variety of delicious salamis and *coppa* (air-dried neck of pork).

Here are a few rewarding eating places in **Montu'Beccaria**: the **Al Pino – Da Mario Sopra Stradella** (Tel: 0385/60479, closed Tuesday afternoon and Wednesday), the **Canneto Pavese da Bazzini** (Tel: 0385/88018, closed Tuesday) or the **Stradella Ristorante Italia** (Tel: 0385/48158; overnight accommodation in comfortable, clean rooms), famed for its *brasato* (pot roast) and its *tortelli*.

13. Bergamo

A visit to one of Italy's finest towns, home of Donizetti and of the Condottiere (military leader) Colleoni (1400–75).

— By car; distance 130km (80 miles); duration 1 day —

It's quite possible to take a bus (departing from the Piazza Castello) or a train (from the Stazione Centrale) to get to Bergamo, but as you're probably used to the car by now, why not simply take the Milan–Venice motorway and leave it almost exactly one hour later at the exit marked **Bergamo**.

Bergamo Alta

This town has had quite a chequered history: at first it was a free Imperial city (having joined in the fight against the Emperor Barbarossa), then it was ruled by the Visconti, and subsequently spent 400 years as part of the Venetian Republic – which explains the numerous lions of St Mark you'll find all over the city.

On arrival in Bergamo you can either leave your car in the *Autosilo* (multi-storey) in **Bergamo Bassa** (Piazza Giacomo Matteotti, near the Town Hall) or at the Piazza della Repubblica, in the Viale Vittorio Emanuele. From here you can walk to the *Funicolare* (funicular) terminus, situated just where the Viale Vittorio Emanuele bends, and travel up to the upper part of the city in style. Or, if you prefer, you can always park the car in front of the church of S Agostino and then stroll up along the Via Porta Dipinta, with *palazzi* to the right and left. The 13th-century Romanesque church to the left, S **Michele al Pozzo Bianco**, contains fine frescoes by the 16th-century Venetian painter Lorenzo Lotto.

Santa Maria Maggiore

As you continue uphill, the city's mighty defensive walls, built during the Venetian period, come into view: the Venetian Republic turned the city into a fortress, controlling an area that extended as far as Valtellina on the southern reaches of the Alps, with its access to the Lombardy Plain. Bastions and towers loom up on all sides, and you finally reach the **fortress** proper and the **Piazza Vecchia**, the imposing centre-piece of **Bergamo Alta** (*alta* meaning 'high', because it is nearly 400m/1,300ft above sea level). Visible from a long way off, this old part of the town is largely traffic-free and is almost unchanged since the Renaissance.

At the other end of the square is the old 12th-century **Palazzo della Ragione** with its elegant portico and Gothic triforium – sporting the lion of St Mark, naturally. The most famous buildings in the city are on this square: the **Duomo**, which has a fresco by Tiepolo in its apse, and **Santa Maria Maggiore**, a picturesque and complex 12th-century Romanesque building sporting magnificent portals. Opposite the presbytery is the tomb of the great opera composer

Gaetano Donizetti, and also the 14th-century **Colleoni Chapel** (designed by the architect Amadeo), which is the last resting place of Bartolomeo Colleoni, the great *condottiere* (military leader) under the Venetians.

Leave the church and make your way to the nearby **Piazza Mascheroni**, taking in a small detour on the way to visit the **Museo di Donizetti** in the Via Arena. Then, in the Piazza, there's the **Cittadella** with its mighty tower (formerly the residence of the Venetian governors). Passing under a large archway, you'll come to an open square called **Colle Aperto**, enclosed by the 16th-century **Porta S Alessandro**. It's here that the walk up to the **Colli di S Vigilio** (461m/1,500ft above sea-level) begins. There's a ruined castle up there, and I assure you it's worth the climb for the fantastic view of gently-sloping vineyards and magnificent villas spread below.

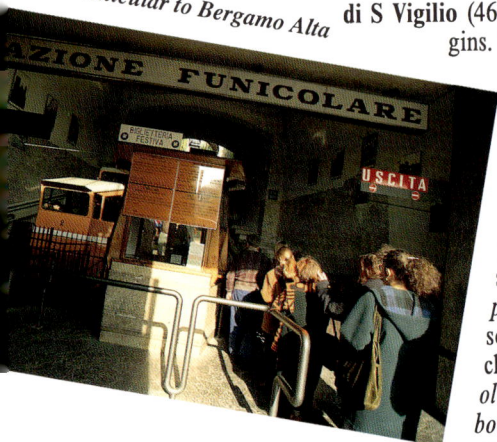

Funicular to Bergamo Alta

Walking certainly does improve the appetite, though. The specialities of this area include *polenta* (maize porridge) with songbirds, or with butter and cheese, *polenta* with sausage, *ravioli al burro* (butter ravioli), *vitello bollito* (boiled veal) and *cuore di vitello alla brace* (grilled calf's heart). The following restaurants, all in Bergamo Alta, are definitely worth a visit: the rustic **Taverna del Colleoni**, Piazza Vecchia (expensive); **La Pergola**, Borgo Canale 82, which has a terrace and a great view; or the cosy **Agnello d'Oro** (Via Gombito 22), with overnight accommodation in the 17th-century *palazzo*.

After eating, you can either walk back to the Piazzale S Agostino and drive down to **Bergamo Bassa** in the car, or descend in the funicular. Once you've arrived in the lower part of the town, go down the Via Pignolo until it connects with the Via S Tomaso, at the end of which you'll find the **Pinacoteca dell'Accademia Carrara** (open 9.30am–12.30pm, 2.30–5.30pm). The picture gallery contains priceless works by such great masters as Pisanello, Botticelli, Mantegna, Carpaccio, Rubens, Velasquez, Dürer, Tintoretto, Tiepolo and Lotto.

Lotto was a 16th-century Venetian painter who settled in Bergamo. He was known in particular for his perceptive portraits and mystical paintings of religious subjects. If you like his work, you may want to make a detour to **Trescore** and on from there to the **Villa Suardi**, 15km (9 miles) further on, where the small 14th-century church of **S Barbara**, situated in the gorgeous villa park, contains frescoes by Lotto – and the A4 motorway back to Milan is just a stone's throw away.

Eating Out

Unlike many other big Italian cities, Milan still retains its own, traditional style of cuisine, and its history can be traced right back to the Lombards. It reflects the common-sense approach of the people here: food should be good, of course, but without being unnecessarily flashy and trashy. At a recent meeting of Milanese epicures a new phrase was invented: *Slow Food*. Coined to describe dishes whose preparation needs time and attention, this was a conscious reaction to dull, uninspiring fast food as well as unreliable *nouvelle cuisine*.

Slow food means Milanese specialities: *risotto alla milanese* (with the characteristic saffron), *costoletta* or *costoletta alla milanese, osso buco* (stuffed leg of veal), *cassoeula* (pronounced 'cassoo-urla', a very filling pork and cabbage stew) and *panettone* (cake with lemon rind and sultanas added) – to name only a few.

Of course, Milan contains restaurants to suit every palate and wallet: from self-service establishments, pizzerias and unpretentious *osterie* to the very numerous Tuscan *trattorie* with their good and relatively inexpensive food – and of course there are also the *Guide Michelin* gourmet temples.

But back to the Milanese specialities. Yellow risotto (also referred to as *risotto alla milanese* or *risotto con lo zafferano*) derives its name from its inventor, a young man called Zafferano (Saffron) in 1574. This aspiring fellow was a glazier, and liked adding a dash of saffron to his colour mixes in order to produce the shiny silvery-yellow for the windows of the Duomo (the Cathedral). This is apparently what inspired him to 'gild' the risotto he'd made his wife for their wedding day.

The recipe? I can give you the real live original recipe to serve four, dating from 1821:

The Milanese yellow risotto

Trattoria Vecchia Milano

take 8 or 9 handfuls of rice, 30 grams (1oz) of butter, 30 grams (1oz) of beef marrow or 2 teaspoons of dripping or – if you really must – 1 or 2 stock-cubes. You need 1 litre (2.1 pints) of stock, at any rate. Then a touch of saffron, 1 small onion, 20 grams (¾oz) of dried mushrooms, and lots of (preferably fresh) Parmesan cheese. First, soak the mushrooms in lukewarm water, then dice the onions and fry them gently in the butter. Now add the marrow (or the dripping), then fry the rice with the onions briefly and give the whole thing a good stir. Now add the mushrooms and, little by little, the stock. When the rice is ready to eat you add the saffron, the grated Parmesan and the butter, and mix it all up together. *Buon appetito!*

And now the *costoletta alla milanese*: this is often referred to as a 'remake' of the Wiener Schnitzel, a misconception dating from the time when Milan was part of the Austro-Hungarian empire. Actually it's far more likely that Governor Radetsky tasted it for the first time in Milan and was so impressed that he took it back to Vienna with him. The genuine *costoletta milanese* is coated with egg and then fried in butter!

The *cassoeula*, by way of contrast, is a colourful mix of pork rib, pigs's trotter and cabbage, not for the squeamish, that's for sure. *Ossobuco* and tomato go hand in hand, though – but make sure it's always knuckle of veal! Then all you need is an uncorked bottle of *Barbera*... Cheers!

Key to prices

Expensive: 100,000 lire or more per person.
Moderate to expensive: 60,000 lire or more per person.
Moderate: Around 50,000 lire per person.
Inexpensive: Around 25,000 lire per person.

To check over 150 menus available in Milan's restaurants, access the Internet at: http://www.gpa.it Or you can fax 39-2-6684726 or get a copy of *Menu Milano*, available from bookshops.

Gourmet Restaurants

BISTROT DI GUALTIERO MARCHESI
La Rinascente (Duomo), Via San Raffaele 2. Tel: 877120
Closed Monday lunchtime and Sunday. Excellent fish and meat dishes with matched sauces and herbs. Expensive but great views over the cathedral.

LA SCALETTA
Piazzale Stazione di Porta Genova Tel: 58100290
Closed Sunday and Monday. Fine seafood and risotto in a dining room decorated with modern art. Navigli quarter. Expensive.

IL TEATRO
Hotel Four Seasons, Via del Gesù 8 Tel: 77088
Evenings only, closed Sunday. Creative cuisine in the heart of the fashion district. Expensive.

Milanese Cuisine

BIFFI SCALA TOULA
Piazza della Scala Tel: 866651
Closed Sunday and Saturday lunchtime. Chic gourmet restaurant by La Scala. Traditional cuisine with a creative twist. Expensive.

BOEUCC
Piazza Belgioioso Tel: 76020224
Closed Saturday and Sunday lunch. A temple of Milanese gastronomy (risotto, veal etc.). Formal. Expensive.

LA NOS
Via Bramante 35 Tel: 3315263/3315363
Closed Monday and Tuesday. Milanese cuisine including *bollito* (boiled meat), *arrosto* (roasts), *filet à la Robespierre*, *torta di mele* (apple pie). Very good service. Moderate to expensive.

L'ULMET
Via Disciplini/Via Olmetto 21 Tel: 86452718
Closed Sunday and Monday lunchtime. Small restaurant with a cosy atmosphere. House specialities include *tegamino di escargot* (fried snails) and *tortelloni di bietola* (with beet). Also offers first-class wine list. Expensive.

OSTERIA CORTE REGINA
Via Rottole 60 (Via Padova) Tel: 2593377
Closed Saturday lunchtime and Sunday. In a converted farmhouse off the beaten track. Fish and pasta specialities. Moderate to expensive.

PECK
Via Victor Hugo 4 Tel: 876774
Closed Sunday. This distinguished temple of gastronomy is linked to the excellent delicatessens of the same name in Via Spadari (see *Pick & Mix 1, page 36;* and *Shopping*). Cool, slightly austere setting near the Duomo; punctilious service. Patronised mainly by business people. Booking advisable. Expensive.

AL PORTO
Piazzale Cantore (Darsena) Tel: 8321481/89407425
Closed Sunday evening and Monday lunchtime. Specialises in fish, including *branzino al pepe verde* (sea perch with green pepper); French white wines and the service are both first-class. Moderate to expensive.

Antipasti at the ready

antipasti and turn-of-the-century interior. *Nervetti* (boiled calf's head with mixed pickles), *pesciolini in carpione* (fish in batter with raisins and wine) and Lombard wines. Moderate.

BICE
Via Borgospesso 12
Tel: 76002572
Closed Monday. Utterly reliable place for *ossobuco*, *crostini* and *saffron risotto*. Moderate.

LE LANGHE
Corso Como 6
Tel: 6554279
Closed Sunday. Piedmontese restaurant offering *brasato al Barolo* (pot roast in *Barolo* wine), biscuits with warm *Zabaione*, first-class wines from the Piedmont region. Moderate.

IL POSTO DI CONVERSAZIONE
Alzaia Naviglio Grande
Tel: 58106646
Closed Monday; also lunchtimes unless booked for a group. In the trendy Navigli (canal) district; cosy, decorated in gentrified rustic style. Offers a creative twist to Milanese favourites. Moderate.

TRATTORIA MILANESE
Via Santa Marta 11
Tel: 86451991
Closed Tuesday. A classic Milanese *trattoria* with nostalgic atmosphere,

American

JULEP'S NEW YORK
Via Torricelli 21
Tel: 89409029
Closed Saturday, only open evenings. Tex-Mex style. Moderate.

MOCAMBO
Via Sant'Agnese 16
Tel: 72004147
Fun, Hollywood-style venue serving American steaks. Moderate.

Brazilian

BERIMBAU
Via de Andreis 13
Tel: 701 02 800
Closed Monday. Food is excellent. Music after 10pm. Moderate. Book.

Greek

MYCONOS
Via Tofane 5,
Tel: 261 02 09
Evenings only, closed Tuesday. Mod.

Japanese

SUNTORY
Via Verdi 6
Tel: 86 22 10
Closed Sunday. Central site. Expensive.

Middle Eastern

ACCADEMIA
Via Accademia 53
Tel: 2891569
Closed Sunday. Kitchen closes at 11pm. Good meat and traditional Lebanese *mezze*. Moderate.

IL FONDACO DEI MORI
Via Solferino 33
Tel: 653711
Tucked into an old *palazzo*, this fashionable Somali restaurant offers dishes from all over the Arab world. Worth paying extra to sit in the tented 'Berber' corner, where dishes are served to guests amongst cushions and tribal rugs. Moderate.

Russian

YAR
Via Mercalli 22
Tel: 58305234
Closed Sunday. Authentic Russian cooking. Trendy. Moderate.

Spanish/Cuban

HAVANA
Via Bligny 50
Tel: 58301327
Closed Sunday. Cuban cuisine and live music. Moderate.

Vegetarian

JOIA
Via Castaldi 18
Tel: 29522124/2049244
Closed Saturday lunchtime and Sunday. First-class vegetarian food served in two rooms (for smokers and non-smokers). Fixed menu. Moderate.

Pizzerie

CALAFURIA
Via dell'Unione 8
Tel: 86462091
Closed Sunday. One of the best places in town for a crusty, traditional pizza. Fairly central. Inexpensive.

PREMIATA PIZZERIA
Via Alzaia Naviglio Grande 2
Tel: 89400648
Closed Tuesday. Lively; summer garden (in the canal quarter). Inexpensive.

Risotto

CASA FONTANA
Piazza Carbonari 5
Tel: 6704710
Closed Saturday lunchtime and Monday. A risotto lover's paradise. Advisable to book. Welcoming. Moderate.

Budget Restaurants

Milan's *paninari* (young people) satisfy their hunger and thirst with sandwiches and beer or coke at the city's

so-called *paninoteche* – at student prices, naturally (around 10,000 lire). I recommend the *paninari* among you to visit the area around the *navigli* (canals), where a lot goes on in the evening.

Or perhaps you'd prefer fast food? On the cathedral square you'll find **VIRGIN MEGASTORE**, which also houses outlets selling pizza, American snacks and Italian ices.

Self-service

There are so-called *tavole calde* all over the place for people in a hurry at lunchtime: the chain called **AMICO DELLA MOTTA**, for instance, where you can just have an ice-cream or drink a cup of tea or *espresso*, is a firm favourite (Via Piazza Duomo 1/Via Orefici). **BREK** is also good, with branches on Piazza Cavour and Corso Italia.

Midnight Dining

The nightlife capital of Italy always has food available for nocturnal prowlers, in restaurants, cabarets, live music bars or piano bars.

AL GARIBALDI
Via Monte Grappa 7
Tel: 659 80 06
Open until 4am, closed Friday and Saturday lunchtime. Garibaldi is a favourite late-night rendezvous point for people from the worlds of show-business, politics and fashion. Offers a pleasant, relaxed atmosphere. Expensive.

BE BOP
Via Col di Lana 4
Tel: 8376972
Open until 4am, closed Sunday and Monday. Young, friendly atmosphere. Pizzas and salads. Inexpensive.

ALFREDO
Via Borghese 14
Tel: 3319000
Closed Sunday; closes between 3 and 4am (depending on clientele). Run by Alfredo Valli, one of the greats of Milan gastronomy. Elegant. Expensive.

TRATTORIA TOSCANA
Corso di Porta Ticinese 58
Tel: 89406292
Open until late but call to check. Closed Sunday. Tuscan dishes served in a charming garden. Moderate.

Something to suit every taste

Snack bars, tearooms. piano bars, pubs, cafés…For the best nightlife head for the Navigli (canal quarter centred on Naviglio Grande and Naviglio Pavese) or the more elegant Brera quarter (metro: Lanza).

AL TEATRO/BAR
Corso Garibaldi 16
Tel: 864222
Open 7pm–2am, closed Monday. The right place to meet up after a theatre evening, Bohemian atmosphere. The place for spotting models or would-be models. Moderate.

BAR GIAMAICA
Via Brera 32
Open until 2am, closed Sunday. Bo-

hemian bar started in the 1960s and still popular with the locals. In the heart of the Brera district.

CAFFE MILANO
Piazza Mirabello 1
Tel: 29003300
Viennese-style café. Good for a quick lunch, aperitifs and cocktails.

CAMPARINO BAR ZUCCA
Piazza Duomo 21
Tel: 86464465
Open until 8.30pm, closed Wednesday. Old-fashioned spot for sipping a campari, while people-watching from the gallery. Also tearooms.

COVA
Via Montenapoleone 8
Tel: 76000578
Closed Sunday. Genteel and prestigious *pasticceria* in the fashion district. Closed Sunday.

GRAND HOTEL PUB
Via A. Sforza 75
Tel: 89511586
Open evenings until late, closed Monday and August. Lively tavern with seasonal dishes, jazz, a *pergola* and an outdoor bowls pitch (*campo da bocce*). Moderate.

VIEL
Foro Bonaparte 71
Tel: 878004
Good *gelateria* opposite the Sforzesco Castle. Sorbets and ice-creams at outside tables in summer.

Piano Bars

Eat your food to the sound of virtuoso solo pianists or small combos:

EL BRELLIN
Via Alzaia Naviglio Grande 14
Tel: 58101351

Open evenings, closed Sunday. Romantic spot by restored wash-house and canal. Milanese menus. Moderate.

CALIMERIUS
Via San Calimero 3
Tel: 58309702
Open 6pm–3am, closed Sunday. Offers quiet, elegant atmosphere. Live music plus first-class snacks and cocktails. Just the place for young lovers. Moderate prices.

ORIENT EXPRESS
Via Fiori Chiari 8
Tel: 8056227
Trendy theme restaurant in the Brera quarter, designed to resemble the famous train. Italian regional cuisine in 'carriages'. Piano bar. Moderate.

Cabaret

Milan has a long cabaret tradition extending back as far as the *Risorgimento* period (mid-19th century). Several famous stars began their careers in Milan, including Dario Fo, Gaber, Franca Valeri and Paolo Rossi. Most of the city's clubs are in the *navigli* (canal) area.

CAPOLINEA
Via Lodovico il Moro 119
Tel: 89122024
Closed Monday. Specialises in satire and music (usually jazz). Milanese and Tuscan cuisine. Moderate.

check). Trendy crowd includes actors, models and students.

Milano Erotica

LA PORTA D'ORO
Piazza Diaz 3
Tel: 863680
Open until 4am. Revues direct from Paris. All things naughty.

Live Music and Shows

IL CALESSINO
Via Thaon de Revel 9
Tel: 6684935
Open 9pm–2am nightly, closed Wednesday. A gentrified rustic-style restaurant and club; traditional Milanese songs and cabaret.

SCIMMIE
Via Ascanio Sforza 49
Tel: 89402874
Open 8 pm–2 am, closed Tuesday. Half *birreria* (pub), half restaurant in a courtyard overlooking barges on the Naviglio Pavese. First-class blues and jazz.

TANGRAM
Via Pezzotti 52
Tel: 89501007
Closed Sunday and Monday. Everything from funk to jazz, and from rock to fusion. Bar snacks and beer.

ZELIG
Viale Monza 140
Tel: 2551774/27001393
Open 9 pm–2 am, closed Monday. Mixture of live music and cabaret. New cyber-café and bar. Summer garden.

COCO LOCO
Via Corelli 62
Tel: 7561226
Closed Monday. Tropical themed evenings and Latin rhythms. Garden and restaurant.

CA' BIANCA
Via Lodovico il Moro 117
Tel: 89125777
International cuisine in 17th-century building. Live jazz and superior cabaret. Moderate.

Discos and Dancing

Given the number of themed nights, ask your hotel receptionist to call the club and check what's on. The following open about 10pm–3am.

BEAU GESTE
Piazza Velasca 4
Tel: 8900692
Open Thursday to Saturday. Part club, part disco. The place for youngish professionals. Strict door policy.

GIMMI'S
Via Cellini 2
Tel: 55188069
Closed Monday and Wednesday. Fairly chic; older crowd. Often live music.

HOLLYWOOD
Corso Como 15
Tel: 6598996
Open late, closed Monday. Popular with fashion and sports stars. Crowded.

SHOCKING CLUB
Bastoni di Porta Nuova 12
Tel: 6595407
Closed Sunday and Monday. Themed evenings include rock and funk (call to

Check through the 'what's on' listings in the major dailies such as *La Repubblica* (on Thursday) or *Corriere delle Sera* (on Wednesday); or you can consult the special list of events published by the city itself, available from kiosks.

Cinema

Most first performances tend to be screened in the cinemas along Corso Vittorio Emanuele and the surrounding area (**Ambasciatori, Gloria, Excelsior**, and also the multiplex **Odeon**). The best place for original-language films is the **Angelicum**; first-run films can be seen at **Centrale 1** and **2** (Via Torino 30) or in **De Amicis** (Via de Amicis 34). For art movies, try the **Cineteca Museo** (Cinema Palazzo Dugnani, Via Manin 2a).

Music

Besides La Scala, the most famous opera house in the world, there's the city-owned **Angelicum** (Piazza S Angelo) with its own symphony orchestra; the **Chiesa di S Marco** (Piazza S Marco 2), where Mozart once lived; the **Conservatorio di Musica Giuseppe Verdi** (Via Conservatorio 12), a former monastery, which stages afternoon concerts; and last but not least the **Musica e Poesia a S Maurizio** (Church of S Maurizio on the Corso Magenta) for ancient and baroque music. In summer, there are lots of outdoor events, including jazz and classical concerts, plays and cabaret on Piazza San Babila; open-air cinema in the courtyard of the Palazzo Reale; and events at the Idroscalo lake, as well as in parks and villas around Milan.

Theatre

Theatres include the **Piccolo Teatro** (Via Rovello 2), founded by Giorgio Strehler and Paolo Grassi, and its offshoot, the **Teatro Studio** (Via Rivoli 6), and the new **Nuovo Piccolo Teatro** nextdoor (the current booking number for all three is: 72333222). The **Dell'Elfo** (Via Ciro Menotti 11) used to be a cinema, and is run by one of Italy's most interesting theatre cooperatives; the **Delle Marionette** (Via degli Olivetani 3b) features Italy's most successful puppet theatre troupe, the Colla brothers; and the **Manzoni** (Via Manzoni 42) is a traditional theatre dating from 1850.

Off-theatre venues for theatre, music, cabaret, dance and cinema: **Ciak** (Via Sangallo 33); **Teatrotenda** MM (in Lampugnano, tel: 33 40 05 51), the Milan rock temple, also known as 'Palatrussardi"; OUT OFF (Via Dupré 4, bus lines 90 and 91), avant-garde; and the rather unusual **Buratto** (Via Mercato 3) which does its own children's productions.

Calendar of Special Events

A wide variety of events take place in Milan almost every day of the year. Notable is the **Fiera di Sinigaglia** which takes place on the banks of the Darsena sui Navigli every Saturday, and the **Mercatone dell'Antiquariato** (last Sunday of every month except for July and August), also on the banks of the Navigli. For information about events in the Trade Fair Centre ring the APT on 72524100. Many of the fairs do not run on set dates so you will need to check locally. For information on art exhibitions pick up the latest copies of *Artshow* and *Milano Mese* from the Tourist Office.

JANUARY

6 January: *Corteo dei Re Magi* (Epiphany). The Procession of the Three Kings is held from the Piazza del Duomo to the Church of S Eustorgio.

FEBRUARY

All month: *Carnevale Ambrosiano* (with masked revellers and parades) and *sfilate di moda*, fashion fairs held in the Trade Fair Centre. The fashion collections may extend to March, including shows held in the designers' own *palazzi* or special showrooms in the city.
End of February: *Borsa internazionale del turismo* (Tourism Trade Fair). More information: Expo Via Londonia 2, tel: 02349841.

MARCH

March/April: *Organ concerts* in S Maurizio and S Simpliciano. A similar series takes place in the autumn.
End of March: *Milanomare,* boating fair held in Segrate.

APRIL

Mid-April: *Mostra di pittura 'l'arte al cielo aperto'.* This unusual open-air art fair has been held in the Via Bagutta since 1963. During its two days in spring and autumn it attracts over 200,000 people. *Festa dei Fiori*, a flower and garden festival on the first or second Sunday

of the month, held along the Naviglio Grande canal.

APRIL/MAY

Sussurri e grida. Literally, 'whispering and shouting' – productions by the city's avant-garde theatres.

Milano Cortili Aperti. 'Open doors': visits to private city courtyards.

Internazionale dell'antiquariato (Trade Fair Centre) – the date can change so check with the tourist office well beforehand.

MAY

Danza a teatro. Dance performances take place in various theatres throughout the month.

Milanese sweet declarations of love

Estate all'idroscalo. Start of the summer festival at the Idroscalo lake with sport, folklore and exhibitions.

Milano Aperta. From May to June and October to November, Milan stages numerous major theatrical events.

First week in May: *Festa del Santo Chiodo.* Masses are held at the Duomo as part of the 'Festival of the Holy Nail.'

Last Sunday in May: *Sagra del Carroccio.* A procession in historic costume. The *palio*, a traditional, heartfelt race, is held in Legnano.

JUNE

First Sunday in June: *Festa dei Navigli.* Folklore, music and entertainment by the *navigli* and the Darsena.

JUNE/JULY

Milano estate. The 'Summer in Milan' festival: cultural events, music, theatre and dance. This is sometimes known as *Milano a cielo aperto* because so many events are held outdoors. Events are held in parks, villas, palazzi and even around the Idroscalo lake outside the city.

Musica nei Cortili. Classical concerts in a selection of Milan's finest courtyards.

AUGUST

Musica in Villa. Concerts held in villas around Milan, in July and early August.

Vacanze a Milano. 'Holidays in Milan' festival, including film shows in the open-air. However, many Milanese leave the city at this time in search of cooler mountain air or beach fun.

SEPTEMBER

La Moda a Milano. Fashion shows and events (if not held in October).

From September onwards there are ballet and concert performances in La Scala (the opera season proper only starts on 7 December).

Italian Formula One Grand Prix: this is held at the Monza racetrack (tel: 039-2482212).

Fish for Christmas

OCTOBER

Mostra di pittura 'l'arte al cielo aperto'. The year's second two-day-long open-air art market in the Via Bagutta.

Milano oltre. Festival of theatre, dance, music and 'more' *('oltre')*. Contact the tourist office for details (tel: 725241) — the festival can alternatively be held in June.

Milano poesia. International poetry festival.

Limitrofie. Latest developments in art, theatre and jazz.

First Sunday in October: *Festa di Chiaravalle* held at the abbey outside Milan.

Last Sunday in October: *Sagra del Tartufo*. This truffle festival takes place in the Via Ripamonti.

The Spring/Summer fashion collections are displayed on the catwalks.

NOVEMBER

Premio letterario Bagutta. One of the most important prize-giving ceremonies in the Italian literary world.

DECEMBER

7 December: *Festa di S Ambrogio*. Festival of the city's patron saint, with processions, masses and markets.

Fiera degli Oh bei, Oh bei. This superior flea market begins on the same day, in the Piazza S Ambrogio.

Also on 7 December, the season opens at La Scala and runs until July.

Third week in December: *Natale in Darsena*. A Christmas market, featuring special events and traditional customs, is held on the Darsena until 6 January.

Natale in Fiera (Christmas at the Fair): a seasonal fair held in the Milan Trade Fair complex.

Shopping

To start off with, let's define our terms: 'shopping' in Milan means the same as it does in any other capital city in Europe, i.e. enjoying a pleasant, relaxed stroll, and giving one's eyes a treat above all, while possibly fulfilling some long-cherished desire in the process. Key shopping areas are the **Piazza del Duomo** and its environs: **Corso Vittorio Emanuele, Via Torino, Via Montenapoleone, Via della Spiga, Via S Andrea, Via Santo Spirito, Via Borgospesso, Corso Buenos Aires, Via Paolo Sarpi, Corso Vercelli** and **Corso XXII Marzo.** You'll find absolutely everything in this section of the map, from the *Rinascente* Megastore to boutiques, sportswear shops, gourmet food outlets, antique shops, gift shops, jewellers, carpet stores... *basta!*

Bookshops (*librerie*)

Since Milan is the capital of Italian publishing, and each publishing house runs its own separate bookstore, you have a huge selection; the greatest concentration of bookshops is in the Galleria V. Emanuele: **Bocca,** Galleria V. Emanuele 2, has excellent art books and is a real treasure trove for book lovers; **Einaudi**, Via Goito 5, is a very popular Milanese bookshop; **Feltrinelli**, Via Manzoni 12, has a very good selection, including a lot of foreign-language literature and international newspapers; **Hoepli**, Via Hoepli 5, is the largest bookstore in Italy, covering 4 floors, with a good assortment of specialist books on management, computing and science; **San Babila**, Corso Monforte 2, is the best address for art books, and the staff are very competent; **Il Polifilo**, Via Borgonuovo 3, is an antiquarian bookshop for rare finds from former 18th-century libraries; **Libreria del Corso**, Corso Buenos Aires 49, is Milan's leading fiction bookshop, very large, with its own conference

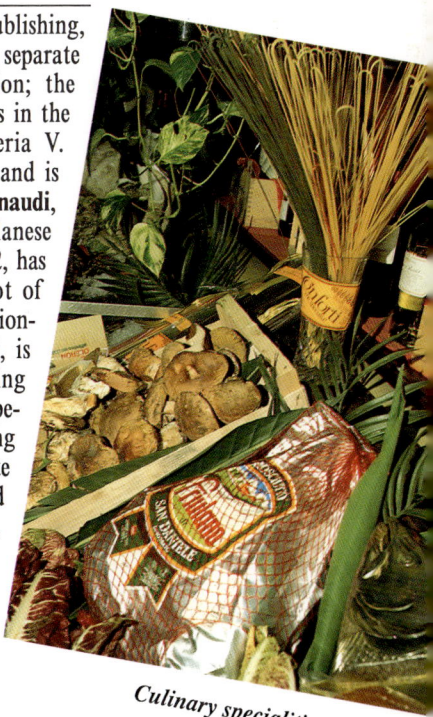

Culinary specialities

terrace; **Rizzoli**, Galleria Vittorio Emanuele 79, sublime atmosphere, travel guides, teaching materials, conference hall; **Mondadori**, Largo Corsia dei Servi 11, is open until 11pm daily.

The city doesn't have all that many foreign-language bookshops. There's **The American Bookstore**, Largo Cairoli/Via Camperio, tel: 878920, where you can find anything in English or American; its rival is the **English Bookshop**, Via Ariosto, tel: 4694468; and there's also the **Librairie Française**, Via S Pietro all'Orto 10.

Children's Shops

Piccolo Lord, Via Plinio 60, is good for baby clothes; the **Benetton** children's outlets are better value than their foreign equivalents.

Delicatessens

You've already had a chance to experience **Peck**, the ultimate in Milanese gastronomy, during your stroll down the Via Torino (see *In Search of Lost Milan, page 36*); fortunately for the taste buds, though, Peck is by no means the only place in town! **Il Salumaio**, Via Monte Napoleone 12, the only establishment in this street that isn't a fashion shop, is filled with gastronomic delights and also has a French and Italian *enoteca* (wine selection); **Parini**, Via Borgospesso 1, estd. 1918, is the place to go for wonderful biscuits and sugar-free cakes, and it also has some 200 different kinds of beer; **Sant'Ambroeus**, Corso Matteotti 7, is the *non plus ultra* of *pasticcerie* and tearooms (why not buy an an ice-cream sculpture, for instance?).

Arte Bianca, Corso Monforte 18, has everything that can be produced using flour, including a huge selection of breads, biscuits and cakes, fresh noodles, ravioli and *focacce* (ultra light flaky pastries with or without all kinds of fillings); **Formaggia**, Via Larga/corner of Santa Tecla, is legendary among Milan's *drogherie*. In particular, it boasts a first-class perfumerie and superb fine wines; and **Leoni**, Corso Venezia 7/1, is a Milanese institution (also open on Sunday) where you can purchase just about everything, including a range of delicious stuffed vegetables.

Design

Milan is the place for modern design, from lighting to home furnishings and furniture. **Gadgets**, Galleria Vittorio Emanuele, sells just that. **Scultura e Design**, Via Hoepli 6, sells some of the best designs, from Murano glass to vases, ornaments, lighting, furniture, rugs and some art. For the finest modern jewellery, try **Bulgari**, Via della Spiga 6, or **Buccellati**, Via della Spiga 22.

Mortadella from the hook

'Drogherie'

These are a Milanese speciality and have absolutely nothing to do with drugs. *Drogherie* are the Italian version of grocers' shops where you can find absolutely everything, from soap to fine whisky and from diet food to mothballs.

Here's a list of the most reasonably-priced ones: **Ferrari**, Via Ponte Vetero 14, has rare balsamic vinegar *(aceto balsamico)*, wines, soap from Marseilles, jams, etc.; **La Coloniale**, Corso Genova 19, has jams, preserves, spirits, washing powder, etc.; **Parini**, Via Borgospesso 1, same as above plus a great assortment of sugar-free cakes and also 200 different kinds of beer (including German *Schaff* beer, fermented in oak casks and sold in numbered bottles) as well as *extravergine* olive oil.

The grace of every living room

Dry Cleaners

Unfortunately there isn't a single 24-hour dry cleaners anywhere in proud Milan. Anyone who doesn't mind parting with his or her favourite item over the lunch-break, though, should visit any of the following *lavanderie a secco* (dry cleaners): **Mack Rapid**, Viale Premuda 34 (open 8.30am–12.30pm and 2.30–7.30pm); **Lavarapido**, Via Tolstoi 15 (open 8.30am–12.30pm and 3.30–7.30pm, express service only on Mondays).

Fashion

Also see *Pick and Mix itinerary 7 – the fashion world.*
Milan has become the capital of the Italian fashion industry. While Rome is still associated with the rather stiff world of *haute couture*, Milan is the focus for the younger, sexier ready-to-wear collections.

The top designers are clustered together on a network of streets. Via Monte Napoleone boasts several Gianni Versace boutiques as well as Gucci, Ungaro, Missoni, Ferragamo, Valentino Uomo and Mila Schön. In Via della Spiga are Krizia and Dolce e Gabbana while Via Sant' Andrea is home to Armani, Ferré, Hermès, Chanel, Moschino, Trussardi and Fendi (furs). Romeo Gigli is in Corso Venezia.

Discount shops offer discontinued lines by the top designers. **Gruppo Italia**, Via Montegani 7a (tel: 89513951), discounts the big names by 30–70 percent (closed Monday morning); **Ciovassino Fashion Discount**, Via Ciovassino (tel: 723012 26), discounts Yves

Saint Laurent and Givenchy; **Minimarket**, Piazza Fidia 3 (tel: 6887418), offers reductions on Ferré and Chanel.

Hats, Luggage, Shoes...

Melegari, Via P. Sarpi 19, does hats for men and women including such brand names as Borsalino, Stetson and Christy's; **Valigeria Brovelli**, Via Vitruvio 38, sells Samsonite aluminium suitcases and fine luggage; **Louis Vuitton**, Via Monte Napoleone 14, is a byword for chic luggage while **Prada**, Galleria V. Emanuele II (also Via della Spiga and Via Montenapoleone), is at the cutting edge of handbag fashion.

    Figus Design, Via Cerva 14, is one of the best leather shops in town; **Il Passatempo**, Via Montevideo 9, is very exclusive; **Borsalino**, Corso Vittorio Emanuele 5, is *the* international place to shop for fabulous hats; **Di Varese**, Corso Vittorio Emanuele 9, is one of the oldest and most respected shoe shops in Italy; **Bruno Magli**, Via Orefici and elsewhere, is famous for shoes and handbags; **Mandarina Duck**, Corso Vercelli and other outlets, has prestigious bags and luggage.

Records, Tapes & CDs

Milan is the capital of the Italian music publishing world, and the publishing house of **Casa Ricordi** looks after some of the best international musicians (and also owns the rights to Verdi's entire opus). **Virgin Megastore**, Piazza Duomo 8 (tel: 72003354) is one of the most central places for music fans, and is open until midnight; **Messaggerie Musicali**, Galleria del Corso 2, does musical instruments, scores and books on music; **Buscemi**, Corso Magenta 31, is a favourite haunt of Anglo-American hi-fi music fans; **The Black Saint**, Via Monti 41, is an almost inexhaustible treasure trove for jazz fans; **Metropolis**, Via Padova 104, is a rock music centre; and **Il Discomane**, Alzaia Naviglio Grande 36, is a second-hand shop with some very rare records.

Milan's second-hand bookshops are always worth a look

Second-hand

Looking for that unbelievable bargain? A tailcoat, cloak or dinner jacket? Then drop in at **Baule**, Via Vetere 13, or try **Surplus**, Corso Garibaldi 7. You want even *more* of a selection?! Well, in that case the place to go is definitely the **USA Shop**, Via San Maurilio 2, with its 20s clothing, Marlene Dietrich-style hats, punk and new-wave outfits, etc.

Sports Goods

Sporty visitors will need the right clothes to compete with the Milanese. Fitness centres, swimming pools and tennis courts have proliferated in recent years. In addition, the Milanese consider the weekend sacred and like to spend it in the countryside, if they can afford to. (They go skiing in the Aosta valley, surfing on the Adriatic, sailing on the lakes and rowing on the Idroscalo).

Brigatti, Corso Vittorio Emanuele 67, with its huge selection of sports goods from golf clubs to baseball masks, is the place to go for Milan's 'in' set (though the prices aren't all that sporting); **Peter Sport**, Piazzetta Liberty 8, right next to the Duomo, does interesting diving gear and also racquets, bags etc. in all sizes and colours at reasonable prices; **Italo Sport**, Corso Vercelli 11, does absolutely everything, though it's expensive; **Sport Fortuna**, Foro Buonaparte 57, does fitness accessories, and skiing, tennis, swimming, hunting and fishing equipment; and **Germani Sport**, Corso Vercelli 3, does everything too, including the strips of major Italian football teams.

Milan's Markets and Supermarkets

I will spare you details of the so-called *ipermercati* (there's one in Milano Fiori that's as large as the Piazza del Duomo). Then there are the *supermercati*: **Esselunga**, with 25 branches, is the best chain. The handiest place for food is **Supercentrale** in the Central Station (open 7.30am–midnight). As far as department stores are concerned, the most famous one is **La Rinascente**, next to the Duomo, which has French-style display windows and a restaurant with panoramic views.

More typical of Milan, however, are the traditional markets – known as *mercatini all'aperto* and *mercatini comunali* – of which the city has around 11,000 altogether. You can find out when and where they are taking place by checking the newspapers (*Corriere delle Sera* on Wednesday or *La Repubblica* on Thursday). Traditional markets include the **Fiera di Sinigallia** at the Darsena dei Navigli, where all manner of bric-a-brac is sold all day long on Saturday, and the **Mercatone dell' Antiquariato**, which has the flavour of a Milanese folk festival; it is held along the Naviglio Pavese and the Naviglio Grande on the last Sunday in the month (except during July and August), and on Via Fiori Chiari on the third Saturday in the month (Brera district).

The *mercatini comunali* take place in various quarters of the city and there you can find food, household equipment, fish, etc. These markets are very popular with the Milanese, not least because of the very reasonable prices charged (market hours are 8.30am–1pm and 4–7.30pm). I would personally recommend the *mercatino* in the Piazza XXIV Maggio, because of the phenomenal selection.

Practical Information

When to Visit

The climate in Milan, like that of the Lombardy Plain as a whole, is damp the whole year through – hot and sticky in summer, hazy and foggy in winter. The horizon is generally grey, and good visibility is rare. Don't let that discourage you, however, because after all, it's the people who make the place. If you're lucky with the weather, though, you'll experience superb days in spring and in late autumn. That's when the Alps seem to be right under your nose from the roof of the Duomo, with visibility extending as far as Monte Rosa.

I'd recommend you to visit Milan at the end of April or the beginning of May, when windy days ensure that there's good visibility. In July and August, the city is virtually empty because everyone is on holiday (a lot of restaurants and shops are closed at this time too) and the weather is unbearably hot and muggy. September, when the city gradually gets back into its brisk stride, has its own special charm.

Arrival by Car

'Gridlock' is another Milanese speciality. Rule number one for anyone who wants to save himself endless stress and trouble is leave your car in the hotel car park (usually a costly option however). The city can quite easily be explored via the public transport system.

The **Azienda Trasporti Municipalli** (ATM), the municipal transport system, has a series of supervised car parks along the major arterial roads leading into the city. Electronic signboards give information on the nearest car parks and how many spaces are left. Thus, anyone arriving via the motorways can park at the various public transport termini (eg of the *metropolitana* Metro system).

There are many ways of reaching Milan, and it's worth summarising them briefly:

Anyone approaching Milan from the south (from Bologna/Rome) arrives in the city along the *Autostrada del Sole*, while the *Autostrada Torino/Venezia* brings in travellers from the west (Turin) and the east (Venice). From Genoa, to the south-west, there is the *Autostrada di Genova*, and from the lakes to the north there is the *Autostrada dei Laghi* (Como/Varese).

A1: *Autostrada del Sole*; from and to Bologna and the Adriatic coast.

A4: *Autostrada Serenissima*; from and to Bergamo, Brescia, Verona (connecting on to the Brenner Pass), Vicenza, Padua, Venice (connecting on to Vittorio Veneto, Pordenone, Udine and Trieste).

A4: From and to Turin, connecting with the Aosta valley.

A7: From and to Genoa and the Italian Riviera. In the city it's a normal street, then it separates into three motorway sections as far as the Swiss border.

Superstrada No 36: Lecco, Sondrio, Valltellina. Connection on to Monza if you're coming from the A4.

Tangenziale Est: This feeder road to the east connects Metanopoli and Linate (the airport) with the south of the city (connecting on to the Autostrada del Sole).

Tangenziale Ovest: Feeder road to the west, connecting the south (connection to *Autostrada del Sole*) with the northbound A8, via the Porta Ticinese and San Siro.

Tangenziale A4 Turin/Venice: The motorway acts as a feeder and provides a connection with Monza via the Viale Zara. In Agrate it joins the Tangenziale Est and continues on to Venice. A word of warning, though: permanent road works, hopeless overcrowding and bad signposting (even Rome's *raccordo annulare* pales in comparison) have turned the *tangenziali* into a veritable nightmare for foreigners.

Assuming you've found your way into Milan, you now need to find somewhere to park. The information office of the ATM can help you further (tel: 890197 or 6697032, 8.00am–8pm except public holidays) should you experience any difficulties with the following car parks:

Car parks to the northeast: Take the exit on the *Autostrada Venezia* near the *Tangenziale Est* (A4)

Cascina Gobba: 800 spaces, also open at night (connection: Metro line 2)

Cologno Nord: 500 spaces (connection: Metro line 2)

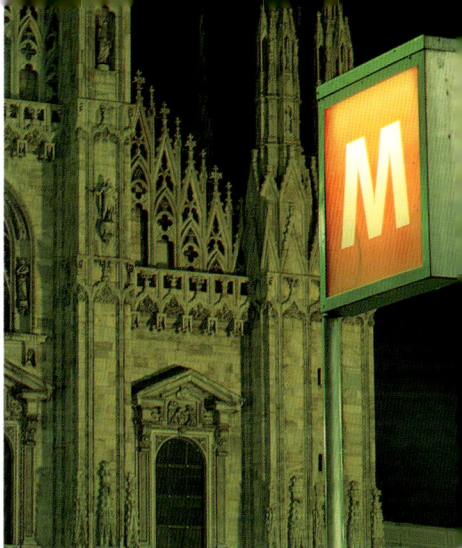

Crescenzago: 600 spaces (connection: Metro line 2)

Forlanini: 650 spaces (connection: Tram 12 and bus 73 to Linate airport, and the Metro system)

Gessate: 500 spaces (connection: Metro line 2)

Car parks to the north: Near the *autostrada* A4 to Venice and the Autostrada dei Laghi junction (A8, A9).

Sesto Marelli: 250 spaces (connection: Metro line 1)

Lampugnano: 2,200 spaces, also open at night (connection: Metro line 1)

Molino Dorino: 450 spaces (connection: Metro line 1)

Car parks to the south: On the *Tangenziale Ovest* and at the exit from the *autostrada* from Genoa (A7).

Romolo: 250 spaces (connection: Metro line 2)

Bisceglie: 900 spaces; closed 10pm–7am (connection: Metro line 1)

Private car parks in the city centre:
Autosilo Repubblica: *Piazza Repubblica 14*, 24 hours.

Autosilo Diaz: *Piazza Diaz 6 (very close to the Duomo)*, open 7.30–1am.

Autosilo Gorizia: *Via Gorizia 14 (on the Darsena dei Navigli)*, open 6.30–1.30am.

Autosilo Nerino: *Via Nerino 6*, 24 hours (tel: 8056725).

Petrol stations that are open at night include:
AGIP: Piazzale Accursio, 10pm–7am; Viale le Marche 32, 10pm–1am.
Esso: Viale Liguria 12, 10pm–7am; Piazzale le Baracca, 10pm–1am.

By Train

Anyone arriving by train in Milan will arrive at the Central Station (Stazione Centrale), the Stazione Piazza Duca d'Aosta, the Stazione Garibaldi or the Stazione Lambrate. Metro lines 1 and 3 will then take you into the centre and to the Piazza del Duomo.

The central station was given a facelift for the World Cup in 1990. The platforms are up on the first floor, where you can also find Travel Information (tel: 63711), a bank (Banca delle Communicazioni, open 8am–2pm Monday to Saturday) and a 24-hour pharmacy (tel: 669 07 35). There's also a self-service here if you're feeling hungry (11.30am–10pm), and a supermarket (open late).

The Milan City Tourist Office (open 8am–7pm) is in the gallery off the departures hall. The Albergo Diurno ('day hotel', open 7am–7pm) can provide you with a quiet room, luggage service, a bar, hairdresser, manicure and pedicure service, drugstore, dry cleaning service (it takes a day though), photocopier, bath, showers and toilets. Next to the tourist office (where you can get train tickets without having to queue) is the post office.

By Plane

Milan has two main airports: the international one, **Forlanini Linate**, and the intercontinental one, **Malpensa**. In emergencies, or if it's foggy, there's a third one too: **Orio in Serio**, near Bergamo.

Linate lies about 8km from the centre (about 30–35,000 lire by taxi).
General Information: tel: 748522 00
Domestic Arrivals: tel: 28106202
International Arrivals: tel: 28106310
International Departures: tel: 2810 6324/28106306
Lost and Found: tel: 70124451
Car Hire at the Linate:
AVIS: tel: 717214
EUROPCAR: tel: 761102 58
HERTZ: tel: 70200256
Getting to Linate airport: There is a shuttle bus operated by the Municipal Bus Service (STAM). This runs every 20–30 minutes from the central station, from 5.40am until 9pm. The ATM bus no. 73 travels regularly (5.30am–midnight) from the front of the airport (Piazzale del Aeroporto) to its terminus on the Piazza S Babila/corner of Corso Europa.

The airport at **Malpensa**, a full 40km (25 miles) from the city centre, is reached by bus or a metro/bus link:
General Information: tel: 74852200
International Departures: tel: 268006 27/26800613
Lost and Found: tel: 74854215
Car Hire at Malpensa:
AVIS: tel: 40099375
EUROPCAR: tel: 40099351
HERTZ: tel: 40099022
Getting to Malpensa airport: The simplest way is to catch the 'Airpullman' bus which leaves (on the hour and every half-hour) from the Airpullman office outside the Central Railway Station. Tickets cost 13,000 lire and the journey takes an hour. Alternatively, take the metro to Lampugnano Air Terminal and pick up the Airpullman bus there (bus journey takes 30 minutes). Tel: 66984509 to check times.

Most banks open from 8.30am–1.30pm and 2.15pm–3.45pm. Almost all of them have exchange facilities. The Banca delle Communicazioni in the Stazione Centrale is open longer as are several *bureaux de change* on the platforms. You can also try a 'dispenser', or change machine: they turn foreign currency into lire but not the other way round. At Linate Airport the Banca Popolare di Lodi and the Banca Popolare di Milano are open daily from 8am–9pm. The same conditions apply to the Banca Popolare di Milano at Malpensa Airport.

USEFUL INFORMATION

Geography & Topography

Milan, 122m (400ft) above sea level, is the capital of the province of the same name, and also the largest archbishopric in the world.

In 1997 the population within the municipal borders continued to decrease to below 1.4 million. But Greater Milan – made up of 105 municipalities covering 1,224 sq km (470 sq miles) – has a population of over 4 million. It also produces around 25 percent of Italy's GNP, and one quarter of Italy's industry plus countless service industries are based here too.

Milan developed in a series of rings around its historic Roman core. The Roman centre is encircled by the Spanish walls, and around them are the *bastioni*, the outer ring-roads (the bus lines out here are 96 and 97, and tram 29 – see *Pick and Mix* routes 2 and 4).

Weather & Views

In Milan in summer the temperature averages 26-28°C (78-82°F), and in winter 5-11°C (41-52°F). Winter fogs can last an unusually long time, often up to 15 or 20 days a month. The rare breezes tend to come from the southwest. In December and January the sky is usually completely overcast, and it rains sporadically. Snow is very rare. Humidity is high all year round, as elsewhere in the Lombard Plain.

The one place to get an aerial view of Milan is the roof of the Duomo (tickets on sale just outside the Duomo, 9am–5.30pm). There's a lift up to the roof in the right transept; however, you can view the cathedral in more comfort from the restaurant at the top of Rinascente department store.

Tourist Information

The **Milan Tourist Information Office** (tel: 725241) has an office in the shopping gallery on the platform level of the Central Station (open Monday to Saturday 8am–8pm). The Municipal Railways have a **tourist office** here too: **Ferrovie dello Stato** (tel: 67 5001).

Next to the Duomo is the main tourist office for Milan and the surrounding district, the **Azienda Promozione Turistica** (APT – Via Marconi 1, tel: 725241; fax: 72524250). Here you can pick up the *Milano Mese*, a guide to events in Milan, or *Milan is Milan*, an audio-guide to sights and museums. You can also enquire about city bus tours (which usually leave from outside the tourist office).

If you're planning to be in Milan for a couple of weeks, it's worth getting the *Pagine Gialle Turismo* (Tourist Yellow Pages) from Telecom Italia offices (it's free).

Maps

Maps of Milan are available from all stations and airports as well as newsagents and kiosks. They are also obtainable from the tourist information centres (APT) in the Central Station and at Via Marconi 1, as well as from travel agents. Ask for maps showing the public transport system from the transport information office at the Duomo metro station.

City Round Trips

The **Tourist Information Office** at the Central Station (tel: 725241) or at Via Marconi 1, organises individual or group trips at varying prices. Guided tours can be booked here, including the good Autostradale City Tour. This is a (multi-lingual) 3-hour-long round trip by bus, beginning at the Piazzetta Reale alongside the Duomo (departing at 9.30am). Bus tours include 'Milan Art Tours' which visit the historic towns of Pavia and Vigevano at weekends (book at the tourist office).

Public Transport

We definitely recommend the use of public transport for our various tours and trips in this guide: driving in Milan means queues, stress and very few parking spaces (and the multi-storeys are expensive).

The offices of the **Azienda Trasporti Municipali (ATM)**, located at the Metro stations 'Duomo' and 'Stazione Centrale', have all the information you'll need, tel: 89010797.

Tickets & Regulations

You can buy tickets at all Metro stations, newsagents and automatic vending machines, and also in the city's *bar tabacchi* (bars that sell tobacco) displaying a yellow sign; several kiosks also offer this service.

The **hour-long ticket** *(biglietto ordinario)* can be used for a (generous) period of 75 minutes on all forms of transport, but only once in the Metro. The tickets (costing 1,500 lire) need to be stamped in the machines you'll find on the trains and buses.

Then there's the **24-hour ticket**, the **2-day ticket**, a **weekly ticket**, and a good value **Carnet** with 10 tickets for 14,000 lire; their prices tend to change every few months.

Travelling without a valid ticket can cost up to 30,000 lire in fines.

Children under 1m (3ft) in height travel free, while dogs are only allowed with muzzles.

Taxis

The taxis in Milan are generally white (at the Central Station, unauthorised taxi drivers will call out to you, trying to entice you to step inside their vehicles – do not do so on any account). Across the whole city you'll always find a cab at the taxi ranks, which are on most main streets. There's a comprehensive list of ranks in the *pagine gialle* (yellow pages).

In an emergency you can ring a radio taxi, and the following should normally turn up:
Ambrosiana Radio Taxi: tel: 5353
Arco Radio Taxi: tel: 6767
Auto Radio Taxi: tel: 85 85

dolomiti sport

LA MONTAGNA LA TROVI A DUOMO.

Esperia Radio Taxi: tel: 83 88
Taxis are quite expensive, with a minimum charge of 8,000 lire and surcharges for night-time, holidays and luggage.

Hire Cars

Leave the hire car behind while sightseeing in the city (the city centre is closed to all non-foreign registered cars between 7am and 7pm).
AVIS
Centre, tel: 6690280
EUROPCAR
Linate airport, tel: 76110258
Centre: Piazza Diaz, tel: 86463454

Cycling

The best advice for those planning to explore Milan by bike is don't. The car is king in Milan, and it spares neither pedestrians nor cyclists. If you really feel like cycling, there are a few things you should know: the city has 23km (14 miles) of cycle lanes, but, although well laid out, they're usually totally blocked by parked cars or bags full of rubbish.

A popular transport scheme allows cyclists to take their bikes on the metro at weekends. This means you can cycle to the lovely abbeys and villas outside Milan (see page 57). Ask for the *Metro Più Bici* (metro plus bike) brochure available from the transport office at the Duomo metro station (tel: 89010797).
Bicycle hire: Bikes can be hired in the city centre at the Piazza Fontana, Piazza San Babila, Piazza Cadorna, Piazza Oberdan, Corso Garibaldi, Largo Cairoli, Piazza S Eustorgio (Monday to Friday 9.30am–6pm). Rental prices are usually reasonable; bring your passport along too for identification.

A good place to cycle is the Parco di Trenno in S Siro, or around the Parco Sempione. Use the maps they

give you when you hire the bike.

And What About Pedestrians?

The rules are the same here as in all other major cities: be extremely careful at traffic lights and zebra crossings (or pedestrian crossings of any description), particularly if you have children with you. Even when the light is green, take an extra look around – and make sure you reach the safety of the other side as quickly as possible. Pedestrian paradise is to be found in the car-free zone around the Duomo as well as the Brera and Via Montenapoleone districts. Plans are afoot to pedestrianise much of the city centre from 1998 onwards.

ACCOMMODATION

If you're planning to stay the night in Milan, expect accommodation problems from the word go. Spontaneous visits can often end up on a park bench, mainly because Milan is almost always hosting some exhibition or other, and whenever it does so the hotels are fully booked.

Hotel reservations are best done via a travel agent before departure. Rooms can also be obtained via the APT information office, Via Marconi 1 (near the Duomo), tel: 39-2-725241. To book rooms in the Lombardy region, contact UVET: tel: 39-2-48027093; fax: 4390337.

Ask whether breakfast is included in the price. The rates mentioned below are based on double rooms. So here is my list of recommended hotels that still treat their guests like guests:

5-Star & Luxury Hotels
500,000 lire upwards

EXCELSIOR GALLIA
Piazza Duca d'Aosta
Tel: 6785; fax: 66713239
Renovated, one of the best hotels in Milan; elegant yet welcoming. Beside the Central Station.

FOUR SEASONS
Via Gesù 8
Tel: 77088; fax: 77085000
Exclusive (the best hotel in town). Wonderful service and restaurants; fitness centre; unadulterated luxury. Central; set in a converted monastery in the fashion district.

GRAND HOTEL DUOMO
Via San Raffaele 1
Tel: 8833; fax: 86462027
Imposing hotel beside the Duomo.

HOTEL DE LA VILLE
Via Hoepli 6
Tel: 867651; fax: 866609
Gracious hotel in the heart of the Montenapoleone fashion district. The rooms are understated and decorated with period furnishings. Canova Restaurant and discreet, panelled bar; an elegant location for afternoon tea or cocktails. Has a loyal following – it's always full during Milan fashion weeks.

PALACE
Piazza della Repubblica 20
Tel: 6336; fax: 654485
In the centre of town. Renovated, with roof garden and noted restaurant. Business clientele. Golf.

PRINCIPE DI SAVOIA
Piazza della Repubblica 17
Tel: 6230; fax: 6595838
An antique gem, luxury suites, private garage and rooftop pool.

4-Star Hotels
200,000–500,000 lire

BONAPARTE
Via Cusani 13
Tel: 8560; fax: 8693601
Small, discreetly chic. Good restaurant, soothing atmosphere. Beside the Castello Sforzesco.

CENTURY TOWER HOTEL
Via Fabio Filzi 25/B
Tel: 67504; fax: 66980602
Entirely composed of spacious junior suites, this friendly hotel is good value and close to the Central Station.

MICHELANGELO
Via Scarlatti 33
Tel: 6755; fax: 6694232
Very modern hotel near the Central Station with 250 rooms, brunch, conference rooms. Noted restaurant.

RADISSON SAS SCANDINAVIA
Via Fauché 15
Tel: 336391; fax: 33104510
Brand-new, calm. Ideal for business travellers; close to the trade fair centre, La Fiera. Garden and good restaurant.

3-/2-Star Hotels
120,000–250,000 lire

ANTICA LOCANDA SOLFERINO
Via Castelfidardo 2
Tel: 6570129
Situated in the Brera. Charming, fashionable and affordable – hence very popular, so book ahead (always full during major fashion shows). Romantic restaurant, friendly service. Eleven rooms only.

NUOVO BISCIONE
Via S Maria Fulcorina 15
Tel: 8693656; fax: 8056825
City centre; facilities for the disabled; pool. Popular so book ahead.

In the San Siro area. Its facilities include a restaurant, playground and golf.

BAREGGINO
In Bareggio
Caravans and tents.

MONZA
In the park at Monza
Tel: (039) 387771
Open 1 April to 30 September. Caravans, tents, campers; covered swimming pool, bar and grocery store.

Youth Hostels

OSTELLO ROTTA
Via Salmairaghi 2
Tel/fax: 39267095
Guests must depart and return within set times. Maximum stay three nights.

EUROPEO
Via Canonica 38
Tel: 3314751; fax: 33105410
Near trade fair centre. This is one of the few hotels in Milan with a garden and an outdoor pool.

GRAN DUCA DI YORK
Via Moneta 1a
Tel: 874863; fax: 8690344
Near the Pinacoteca Brera in an old *palazzo*. Closed during August.

PALAZZO DELLE STELLINE
Corso Magenta 61
Tel: 4818431
Fine new hotel forming part of the large congress centre; facilities for the disabled. Central location.

SANT'AMBROEUS
Viale Papiniano 14
Tel: 48008989; fax: 48008687
Welcoming and efficient. Situated near Parco Solari. Inexpensive.

Campsites

CAMPEGGIO CITTÀ
Via G Airaghi 61
Tel: 48200134; fax: 48202999

BUSINESS HOURS

Apart from food shops, most of the city's shops are open 9am–1pm and 3.30pm–7.30pm. Nearly all the shops are closed on Monday morning.

EMERGENCIES

In Case of Emergency

SOS **emergency number**: tel: 113
Carabinieri 'pronto intervento' (police emergency aid): tel: 112
Fire Brigade: tel: 115
City Police: tel: 772 71
Emergency Medical Aid: tel: 3883
Ambulance: tel: 118
Traffic Police: tel: 32 67 81
Towed-Away Car Lot (ask for *Ufficio Rimozioni*): tel: 77271

Breakdown Services

ACI **(Automobil Club Italiano)**, tel: 774 51; serious accidents, tel: 44 77
ACI **Breakdown Service**: tel: 116
Autofficina Pavese: Via Naviglio Pavese 10, tel: 58111869.

Medical Assistance

Emergency healthcare: tel: 3883 (*Pronto Soccorso*), 118 (ambulance), 34567 or the hospitals listed below.
Emergency Dental Treatment: tel: 66 982478, 24 hours.

Emergency Pharmacies

24-hour: Piazza Duomo, Via Orefici 2, or Central Station (departure hall, tel: 6690735/6690935).
9pm–8.30am: Bracco, Via Boccaccio 26; Ticinese, Corso S. Gottardo 1; Venezia, Corso Buenos Aires 4; Carrobbio, Corso Genova 23.

Hospital Out-Patient Service

Niguarda: Piazza Ospedale Maggiore 3, tel: 64442496
Policlinico: Via Francesco Sforza 35, tel: 5511655
Fatebenefratelli (eye injuries): Corso Porta Nuova 23, tel: 63634699
San Raffaele: Via Olgettina 60, tel: 26432741
Ortopedico Pini: Piazza Cardinal Ferrari 1, tel: 582961

Lost & Found

City Lost Property Office: Via Friuli 30, tel: 5465299.
Central Station: tel: 67712677
Linate Airport: tel: 70124451
Malpensa Airport: tel: 74854215
Trams, Metro: Via Unione 4, Monday to Friday 8.30am–12.45pm and 2.15pm–5pm, Saturday 8.30am–noon

MEDIA

Newspapers

Every newspaper in Milan contains a supplement or a special page with a list of events. You should either buy *Corriere della Sera* on Wednesday or *La Repubblica* on Thursday: both have excellent listing sections on Milan. Also pick up a current copy of *Milano Mese* from any Milan tourist office – this is a monthly listing of events (exhibitions, music and sport) in the Lombardy area (written in Italian and English). Other useful publications are *Vivere a Milano* (Italian/English/Japanese editions), which features articles on Milanese life and events; *A Guest in*

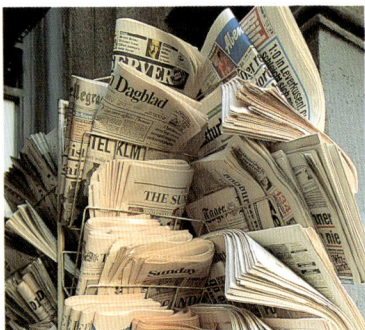

Milan; and *Hello Milano* (both available from large hotels), which list museums.

The main newspapers are *Corriere della Sera* and *Repubblica*. *La Repubblica* certainly has the biggest services section (not on Mondays).

Television

The TV market in Italy is shared between public stations (RAI 1, RAI 2, RAI 3) and private ones. There are a huge number of private stations, many of which, however, are of national importance, e.g. Berlusconi's stations (Italia 1, Rete 4 and Canale 5). The main local stations in Milan are Telelombardia, Lombardia 7 TV, Telenova, Telereporter and Antenna 3.

Radio

There are 170 radio stations sharing the ether above Milan. Since there's no law governing transmission frequencies the stations often tend to overlap. The result? Total chaos. Here's a brief list of the more audible ones: Radio Popolare (107 MHz) is a 24-hour news station; Radio Montestella (103.2 MHz) is a mixture of news and music.

POST & TELECOMMUNICATIONS

Telephoning

The area code for Milan is 02.

Most phone boxes have been changed over to the card system now, and cards *(una carta telefonica)* can be bought in *bar tabacchi* or at news-stands. Most telephone numbers have been changed recently, so call directory enquiries (tel: 12) if you have problems.

To dial other countries, first dial the international access code 00, then the country code: Australia (61); France (33); Germany (49); Japan (81); Netherlands (31); Spain (34); UK (44); US and Canada (1). If using a US credit phone card, dial the company's access number below – Sprint, tel: 172 1877; AT&T, tel: 172 1011; MCI, tel: 172 1022.

Public telephones are plentiful at airports, the Central Station, the Galleria Vittorio Emanuele (Telecom Italia office) and the Piazza Cordusio.

Post Offices

The main post office in the city *(posta centrale)* is at Piazza Cordusio 1 (tel: 8692069). Postal services are available weekdays 8.30am–7pm. Registered letters, parcels and *poste restante* can be handed in or collected at Via Cordusio 4 (weekdays 8.15am–noon). There are more large post offices at the Central Station and at the airports.

Milanese letter-boxes are red and have two slots, one for the city and the other for outside. The orange letter-boxes are for letters that need to reach their recipients in the city within one day (or so you hope): this *servizio postacelere* costs extra.

Telegrams, telexes and telefaxes can be sent off and received round the clock. Go to the Posta Centrale, Via Cordusio 4 (near Piazza del Duomo).

SPECIAL SERVICES

For Children

Milan has a great deal to offer old and young alike.

Babysitter service, Via Vittadini 3, tel: 8263845. Babysitters aged between 19 and 50 look after children up to 12 years old. Minimum booking period ranges from 2 hours to whole days and nights (usually 9am–5pm, however). The babysitters look after the children's clothes too.

Città del Sole, Via Dante 13, tel: 86461683. The only really good toy shop in Milan – no electronic toys.

Gog & Magog, Via Canonica 20, tel: 33610468. Educational games, intelligent free-time ideas.

Libreria dei Ragazzi, Via Unione 3. Educational toys.

Motta Baby, Viale Montenero 22. A huge shop with children's furniture.

Jolly Old Toys, Corso Vercelli 2, tel: 48006604. Antique music boxes, dolls and toys.

Nano Blu, Via S Pietro all'Orto 3. Music boxes and china dolls are among the items on sale.

Teatro del Buratto, Via Mercato 3, tel: 86464986. Performances (musicals, puppet shows, etc).

Teatro delle Marionette, Via Olivetani 3b, tel: 4694440. Not to be missed: Gianni and Cosetta Colla's puppets fascinate children of all ages (Grimms' fairy tales, Hans Andersen, etc).

Luna Park Varesine, Viale della Liberazione, tel: 6571149. This mini-Disneyland is not only of interest to children: there's a great smell of doughnuts and very loud disco music.

Luna Park Idroscalo, Via Rivoltana 64, Segrate (on the way to Linate airport), tel: 7560393. Another fairground but also a place with children's activities: children's theatre, watersports, boats around the lake in the Parco Azzurro (also live music).

For Women

Cicip e Ciciap, Via Gorani 9, tel: 877555. Open until 1am. A bar and restaurant just for women, housed in an old Milanese *palazzo*: young students and middle-aged women can gather here unpestered and play the guitar; or they can attend various other courses.

For the Disabled

Lega per i diritti handicappati (Association for Rights of the Disabled), tel: 5452444. All information on provisions for the disabled in Milan is available here. Also **AID**, tel: 5501 7564.

SPORT

In Milan you can engage in practically any sport, where and when you like. Telephone numbers aren't always provided below – just check in the *pagine gialle turismo* (*Yellow Pages*, free from the Telecom Italia offices).

Football

Consider watching a match featuring AC Milan or Inter Milan, two famous teams, at the **Stadio Olimpico**, Via Piccolomini, tel: 48707123 (or 4042 251 for a tour of the stadium).

Boccia is Milan's favourite sport

Boccia (Bowls)

A popular sport in Milan, which has produced several world champions.

Bocciodromo Comunale, Via Candiani 7.

Sports Centres

Lido, Piazzale Lotto 15, tel: 39266100. One of the best centres. Similar to Saini (see *Tennis*).

Gyms and Fitness Centres

Milan boasts a greater number of gyms, health and fitness centres than any other Italian city. The best hotel facilities are at the **Principe di Savoia** and the **Four Seasons** (see *Hotels*). Or consult your hotel for details of the nearest private gym.

Tennis

Saini, Via Corelli 136, tel: 756 12 80. A major sports centre with tennis, roller skating, ice skating, gym, skiing, etc.

Tennis Club Lamber, Via Feltre 100, tel: 26414808.

Canoeing

Canottieri Olona, Via Alzaia, Naviglio Grande 16, tel: 48951211.

Riding

Centro Ippico Borromeo, S Felice, tel: 753 16 26. Outside Milan.

Centro Ippico Ambrosiano, Via San Dionigi 121, tel: 569 53 94.

Golf

Practise your swing with a trainer at the **Palace Hotel,** Via della Repubblica 20, tel: 6336.
Parco di Monza, 18-hole course, tel: (039) 303081.

Indoor Swimming Pools

Indoor pools are open only in winter, and outdoor pools only in summer.
Cozzi, Viale Tunisia 35, tel: 6599703.
Solari, Via Coni Zugna, tel: 4695278.

Outdoor Swimming Pools

Argelati, Via Segantini 6, tel: 5810 0012.
Canottieri Olona (see *Canoeing*): the best pool in Milan.

Jogging ('Footing')

Giardino Villa Litta, 800m (2,624ft) course.
Monte Stella, up and down this artificial mountain near S Siro.
Parco Sempione, 2,240m (7,300ft) through the park.

USEFUL ADDRESSES

Kiosks Open at Night (Edicole)

Corso Buenos Aires 4 (until 2am)
Galleria Vittorio Emanuele (24 hours)
Piazza Oberdan, near the Porta Venezia (24 hours).
Via Larga 3 (until 2 am).

Foreign Cultural Institutes

British Council
Via Manzoni 38, tel: 772221.
Centre Culturel Français
Corso Magenta 63, tel: 4859191.
Goethe Institut Milan
Via S Paolo 10, tel: 76005571.
United States
Piazza S Alessandro 1, tel: 86339451.

Airlines

Air France
Piazza Cavour 2, tel: 77 38 21.

Alitalia
Via Albricci 5, tel: 628 17. International reservations: tel: 268 53.
Austrian Airlines
Piazza Diaz 5, tel: 86461200.
British Airways
Corso Italia 8, tel: 167278278.
KLM
Linate airport, tel: 70003888.
Lufthansa
Via Larga 23, tel: 583725.

Banks/Bureaux de Change

Credito Italiano, *Piazza XXIV Maggio.*
To change money out of hours:
American Express (see below); **Exact,** Departures Hall , Central Railway Station; **Moneyshop,** Via Orefici 2.

Travel Agencies

Train tickets can be booked at most travel agencies.
Ente Provinciale del Turismo
Via Marconi 1.
Helpful for general queries about Milan.
Touring Club Italiano
Corso Italia 10, tel: 8526304.
The place for good advice (and books) on Italian trips.
CIT
Galleria Vittorio Emanuele, tel: 8637 0232, and *Central Station, tel: 6696923.*
American Express
Via Brera, tel: 72003694/876674.
Also a *bureau de change.*

Advance Ticket Sales

La Prevendita, Piazza Duomo in the Virgin Megastore Duomo Centre, tel: 72003370 (Tuesday to Saturday 10am–midnight, Sunday and Monday noon–10pm); **La Biglietteria,** Corso Garibaldi 81, tel: 6598956 and 65901 88, tickets for all types of event, including foreign ones; APT **(Azienda Promozione Turistica),** Piazza Marconi 1, tel: 725241 – the tourist office will take bookings or at least point you in the right direction.

Index

Art & Photo Credits

Photography   Sergio Piumatti and
Pages 10, 11, 29, 30, 46, 47   Scala/Firenze and
12   La Repubblica/Alinari
Publisher   Hans Höfer
Design Concept   V Barl
Designer   Gaia Text, Munich
Managing Editor   Dorothy Stannard
Cartography   Berndtson & Berndtson

Milan's Metro Network

LINEA 1
LINEA 2
LINEA 3
LINEE IN COSTRUZIONE

GESSATE
C.NA ANTONIETTA
GORGONZOLA
VILLA POMPEA
BUSSERO
CASSINA DE PECCHI
VILLA FIORITA
CERNUSCO S.N.
CASCINA BURRONA
VIMODRONE
GOBBA
CRESCENZAGO
CIMIANO
UDINE
LAMBRATE F.S.
PIOLA

COLOGNO NORD
COLOGNO CENTRO
COLOGNO SUD

limite tariffa urbana
limite tariffa urbana

SESTO F.S.
SESTO RONDO
SESTO M.
VILLA S.G.
PRECOTTO
GORLA
TURRO
ROVERETO
PASTEUR
LORETO

LINATE
BUS 73 PER
SAN BABILA
PALESTRO
P.TA VENEZIA
LIMA

CAIAZZO
SONDRIO
CENTRALE F.S.
REPUBBLICA
TURATI
MONTENAPOLEONE
GIOIA

S. DONATO
ROGOREDO F.S.
PORTO DI MARE
CORVETTO
BRENTA
LODI TIBB
PORTA ROMANA
CROCETTA
MISSORI
DUOMO

GARIBALDI F.S.
MOSCOVA
LANZA
CADORNA
CAIROLI
CORDUSIO

S. AMBROGIO
S. AGOSTINO
P.TA GENOVA F.S.
ROMOLO
FAMAGOSTA

PAGANO
CONCILIAZIONE
WAGNER
DE ANGELI
BANDE NERE
GAMBARA

AMENDOLA-FIERA
BUONARROTI
LOTTO
QT8
LAMPUGNANO

(Stadio S.Siro)

MOLINO DORINO
S. LEONARDO
BONOLA
URUGUAY
PRIMATICCIO
INGANNI
BISCEGLIE